Image Guidance

A Tool for Spiritual Direction

Elizabeth-Anne Vanek

*Preface
by
Ewert Cousins*

PAULIST PRESS
New York/Mahwah, N.J.

Grateful acknowledgement is made to the editors of *Emmanuel* Magazine, for allowing me to reproduce excerpts from my articles, "A Different Kind of Knowledge" (October 1989), "Image Power" (April 1990), and "The God Beyond Images" (January, 1992).

I would like to express my deepest thanks to Elizabeth Barry, SCN, for the many hours she spent driving to and from Kentucky to help me with my work on image guidance in Chicago. Her support, flexibility and skills in spiritual companioning have been invaluable.

Library of Congress Cataloging-in-Publication Data

Vanek, Elizabeth-Anne, 1951–
    Image guidance : a tool for spiritual direction / Elizabeth-Anne
Vanek.
      p.   cm.
    Includes bibliographical references.
    ISBN 0-8091-3321-0
    1. Spiritual direction. 2. Imagination—Religious aspects—
Christianity. I. Title.
    BX2350.7.V37   1992
    253.5'3—dc20   92-12970
                                                          CIP

Published by Paulist Press
997 Macarthur Boulevard
Mahwah, NJ 07430

Printed and bound in the
United States of America

Contents

I dedicate this book to the many stories woven through it and to those who have entrusted these stories to me.

May the telling of sacred tales continue to bring enlightenment to all who dare listen to the narrator within . . .

Preface

Our imagination is one of the greatest of human gifts. The artistic imagination has produced masterpieces of culture: the painting and sculpture of Michelangelo, the poetry of Dante. With our imagination we can recover our past and project our future. Through psychotherapy, we have learned that dreams and waking fantasies can reveal our deepest feelings and the direction of our lives. Through the recovery of the classics of spirituality, we can observe countless examples of the role symbols have played not only in scripture interpretation but in the accumulated spiritual wisdom of the human community.

It should not be surprising, then, that our imagination can be a major resource on our spiritual journey. Awakened within a context of faith, it can be an instrument of grace— bringing us in contact with the deeper spiritual levels of our being, activating our centers of spiritual energy, and providing us with discernment for advancement in our spiritual quest.

In this book Elizabeth-Anne Vanek leads the reader into that realm of the psyche where the imagination itself becomes a spiritual guide. She is especially qualified to lead others on this path. A gifted poet herself, she has enriched her writings with an abundance of mythic symbols from our ancient past, and has pioneered in creating an original genre of dramatic poetry derived from scriptural narratives. She is an experienced teacher in the fields of literature and religious studies, as well as a spiritual director of great sensitivity and wisdom. Realizing the power of symbols and the depth from which they arise, she prudently cautions the director to discern the capacity of the directee to assimilate in a balanced fashion the psychic energy that can be released in the process.

In viewing her work, I have come from several different perspectives. For more than ten years I participated in psychological research in the various levels of human consciousness, especially in the light of symbols that emerge from the depths of the psyche. Much of this research proceeded through guided imagery in a fashion strikingly similar to the method she employs. Another perspective comes from my work in translating, editing, and teaching classics of spirituality, with a focus on the role of images and symbols in the spiritual journey. The third is from philosophies and theologies of symbol, especially as these are related to religious art.

From all three perspectives, one can clearly see the significance of Elizabeth-Anne Vanek's work. Her explorations into the psyche reveal the same levels of consciousness that were reached in the psychological research mentioned above. The symbols which emerge in her work resonate with those found in the spiritual classics, and they harmonize with the classical philosophies and theologies of the spiritual traditions. Add to these perspectives her own remarkable creativity and wisdom, and it is clear why she has been able to awaken in others the resources that guided imagery offers to those on the spiritual quest.

Some, however, may feel that the images that emerge in our psyche are arbitrary, mere flights of fancy and not signposts along our spiritual journey. Undoubtedly many images are of this superficial kind. But there are others—springing from the deeper levels of the psyche where the flow of our spiritual energy resides. These are the images that function in the spiritual journey.

Others may feel that our images are purely subjective and not related to the larger objective structures of reality. This problem could be dispelled if we would view symbols within the philosophical-theological worldview that was pervasive throughout most of Christian history and that gives symbols their rightful place. This worldview, called the symbolic universe, can be seen in the following formulation that was current in the twelfth and thirteenth centuries. The universe can be seen through the metaphor of four interrelated books: the book of creation, which is divided into the book of nature and the book of the soul; the book of scripture; and the book of life. Each book reflects the other and can be read in the light of the other. The book of external nature— the realm of sense objects—is reflected in the book of the soul. God has imparted to certain sense objects a spiritual meaning which is manifested in the book of our soul. Thus by reading these symbols in the depth of our soul we can discern their spiritual meaning for the soul's journey into God.

Because of sin, however, the meaning of the book of creation has been obscured. In God's providence we have been given another book, the book of scripture, to assist us in reading the book of creation. The book of scripture itself contains a treasure of symbols, drawn from the book of nature, whose meaning for the book of the soul is clarified. Finally, God has sent us the book of life itself—the Word of the Father, expressed from all eternity as the book of the Father in the inner life of the Trinity. It is this book who is the Meaning of all the other books and who has become incarnate in Jesus of Nazareth to reveal to us this multidimensional spiritual meaning. Thus, by reading in the book of the soul the symbols drawn from the book of nature—supported by faith and guided by grace—we can be led in our spiritual journey toward union with Christ as the book of life in the mystery of the Trinity.

Granted this multidimensional objectivity of the symbolic universe, not all spiritual pilgrims are drawn by symbols. In the maps of the spiritual journeys, there is the kataphatic way and the apophatic way, or the way of symbols and the way of the negation of symbols, the way of words or concepts and the way of silence. Both ways can lead one to union with God. For those who are attracted by their imaginations to the way of symbols, Elizabeth-Anne Vanek's book offers a privileged access to those symbols that emerge from the depths of the psyche and with grace and guidance can lead the spiritual pilgrim toward the goal of the journey.

Ewert Cousins
Fordham University

Introduction

Shortly after I had completed an internship in spiritual direction, I was startled by the discovery that images could function much like dreams in terms of their ability to heal, to guide and to illumine. I was at a workshop on the wounded inner child when this breakthrough happened. The facilitator had asked us to imagine ourselves as young children; then, before I knew it, much of my childhood played itself out before me. Fascinated, I saw event after event as clearly as if each were present tense, and in every situation I saw an extended hand reaching out to comfort and rescue me. When I finally returned to consciousness, I had a new sense of wholeness, a new understanding of God's faithfulness. Then and there I decided to use images not only for personal prayer and teaching, but also in spiritual companioning.

I began with the self, not daring to experiment with anyone else. I discovered, first of all, that the most powerful images are those which surface naturally from the unconscious. One can respond to pre-fabricated images (e.g. a scriptural image or a literary image) intellectually, but it is the authentic image generated by one's unique inner world which speaks most eloquently to the spirit. Like dreams, the image which presents itself seemingly from nowhere is a

1

piece of the self, demanding attention and offering a wealth of information for those who dare risk time and energy. And like dreams, such images can be painful and puzzling, elusive and challenging, inviting and forbidding. Images, I realized, were one way of listening to God.

I allowed myself to be passive in prayer. At times I came to prayer empty-handed and waited; at others I brought with me images which needed further exploration. I sat absolutely still, often cross-legged, breathing rhythmically; I concentrated on the image, without thinking, without analyzing, simply watching and waiting. And the image would begin to unfold, involving me in a surreal world in which even the most trivial event held deep meaning which I understood with my heart rather than with my head. In one experience I was taken to a place of painful alienation from where I was considering removing myself: there was a liturgical celebration in progress, with people smiling, dancing and singing; a person who had hurt me deeply came over to welcome me, and as I looked into his face, I knew that I should stay and not leave after all.

In another experience, I saw a wooden cross vested in a green chasuble—the same cross before which I had knelt on Good Friday, silently offering God my gifts. In a complex sequence of events which I will abbreviate, the cross discarded the chasuble, tugging and pulling at it as though it were an ill-fitting sweater; then the cross raised itself from its roots, revealing a tiny tree, greening and growing in its place, stretching and spreading, thickening, flourishing, laden with luminous fruit—with opalescent pears and gleaming apples. As I marveled at the tree I heard the words, "*You* are the gift." And I understood that I *would* bear fruit, but that the gift of one's love is more significant than anything one can do . . .

Earlier this year that same cross has returned on a regular basis, but this time vested in a white cloth. In one image sequence I became tangled in the cloth and had to break free, but in another the cross offered me the cloth which became bridal veil instead of shroud. I took this as a sign that I was being called to a new stage in my spiritual journey which involved waiting rather than grasping. Interestingly enough, this image kept on surfacing at a time when I was "between" directors; it confirmed for me the "rightness" of a change which was initially distressing. Some months later I came across the identical cross, complete with woman waiting in prayer, painted on the walls of an ancient citadel on the island of Gozo, off Malta. I was startled by the "coincidence."

Perhaps the most dramatic image to date was one which saved my son's life. During prayer one morning I saw clearly the image of a plastic, saccharine Jesus stretching out his hand across turbulent water, standing very still; he was reaching out to what looked like a crude line drawing of a drowning person whose arms were raised above his head and whose mouth was fixed in a scream. I wrestled with meaning but was left uneasy: I could make no sense of what I saw. The next day I took Peter, 13, and Alexia, 11, on our traditional end of summer blueberry picking day which, as always, we followed with a swim at Michigan City, Indiana. The lake was rougher than usual and I warned the children not to go out of their depth, even though they were strong swimmers. I had forgotten the previous day's image but still had a sense of foreboding. I found myself keeping close watch and continually reminded them about staying close to me. Then, without warning, I heard a cry of urgency, "Mom! Peter's drowning!" To my horror I saw my son frantically making swimming motions while being dragged further and further out; he was caught in an undertow. My first impulse was to swim toward him, but I found the waves impossible. The water sucked at my feet, at my legs, like a voracious vacuum cleaner of indescribable strength. I stood still and stretched out my hand, waiting for the swell to toss him within reach. At times our fingers almost met; at others he seemed to be further and further away from me. I remember praying, "Help, God!" I remember Peter saying, "I'm not going to make it, Mom." And then our fingers touched and I pulled him toward me; together we staggered to the shore, feet planted firmly in sand as we resisted the incredible force that seemed so determined to swallow us up. Only later, when we were panting on the sand, too tired to move, did I remember the image of the day before and understand that it had come as a warning, as a gift.

In these and other experiences I have found myself in touch with a powerful reality which has shaped how I think and how I act, how I perceive and how I judge. At times I find myself laughing; at others I am left in tears as I see and feel more than is comfortable. At times images surface easily; at others, when nothing comes, I turn to alternative ways of praying, realizing that perhaps it is a season for me to speak and for God to listen instead. Praying with images plunges me into depths of the self which would otherwise remain hidden; the "themes" of my life gain full visibility and I find myself confronting that which is most significant.

With some trepidation I began to experiment with using what I call "image guidance" in spiritual companioning. From my own experience, I knew that images could unleash powerful emotions and that I would have to be prepared to deal with them within the session. I realized that while I had an immediate grasp of the "meaning" of my own images, I would have to allow directees (I coined the term "seekers") the freedom to interpret theirs; at the same time I (the "guide") would have to be closely in touch with each unfolding image so that I could, in fact, be "useful."

Another concern was whether I would know what to do

with the image once it surfaced. Should I allow it to unravel itself without any prompting? Should I ask leading questions to facilitate the seeker's experience with the image? Should I intervene if the image became too painful and perhaps guide the seeker toward some kind of healing resolution?

It soon became apparent that context was the most trustworthy guide to follow: rather than worry, I should listen; rather than devise appropriate strategies, I should simply respond as my intuition directed me. I discovered that the possibilities were endless. As I have continued to work with others, as I have allowed a trusted friend—Elizabeth Barry, SCN— to work with me, I realize that my work with image guidance has just begun. I see myself standing at the edge of a vast ocean, dabbling my toes in all that is yet to be discovered. I feel energized by what I have seen and heard, touched and tasted. And I am gratified by the responses of those with whom I am working: by affirming the place of images in their own prayer and inner journeying, they encourage me to further explorations, in deeper seas. These explorations have already brought me into exciting territory. Unaware of the many rich resources on the use of imagery in counseling, I began to develop my "own" method. The basic stages of this process (see Chapter 1) involve:

1. allowing the image to surface
2. examining the context from which the image arises
3. emptying oneself through deep breathing and relaxation exercises so that one can attend to the image
4. encountering the image aided by the verbal directions given by the guide
5. dialoguing with the image while sharing with the guide what one has seen, heard and felt
6. returning to "ordinary" consciousness
7. processing the experience with the guide

Though I use image guidance only when it seems appropriate, and not as an end in itself, I have come to appreciate the powerful insights it can reveal in spiritual direction and other counseling contexts. This book records some of my findings and suggests possible applications of the process; it is by no means the final word, nor is it the first word—it is simply a tool which "came" to me from the unconscious and which I am learning to use with wisdom and caution.

1
Background and Method

As I began to share my excitement about image guidance with others, I realized that my language lacked precision. I could talk about the need for the seeker to be in a relaxed, reflective state. I could speak of "tapping into the unconscious" and letting images "show and tell" what was deep below the surface. I could describe how "powerful" such an experience was for both seeker and guide. However, I was only leaving vague impressions about my experimentation. There was nothing in what I had to say which would enable others to draw on—perhaps move beyond—anything that I had learned. Nor was I providing the necessary information for them to make connections between what I was doing and what Jungians had already explored—the use of the active imagination, for example, or dream-reentry techniques. Nor was I fully describing the benefits of image guidance as a tool in spiritual companioning.

While I began monitoring what was actually happening during image guidance sessions, I also embarked on a rigorous course of reading. I found that, in fact, there are striking parallels between image guidance and active imagination. Both processes originate from the same source:

To bring an emerging unconscious content into consciousness, the immaterial must be clothed in matter, the disembodied, or better the not-yet-embodied, must undergo incarnation; a spirit must be caught in some discernible form in order to become a content of consciousness. . . . Dreams perform this function as do active imagination and other forms of imaginative creative expression. Our text says it is the Philosopher's Stone which performs the transformation of spirit into image. This corresponds to the old statement that dreams come from God. In other words, the image-making power of the psyche derives from its transpersonal center, the Self, and is not a function of the ego. (Edward F. Edinger, *Ego and Archetype* 285)

Both processes also involve "conscious participation" in the imaginative experience:

This kind of imagination is active because the ego actually goes into the inner world, walks and talks, confronts and argues, makes friends and fights with the persons it finds there. You consciously take part in the drama of your imaginations. . . . The "I" must enter into the imaginative act as intensely as it would if it were an external, physical experience. Although it is a symbolic experience, it is still a real experience involving real feelings. (Johnson, *Inner Work* 140–141)

At the same time, however, I also learned that active imagination is usually a solitary task, even though Jungian analysts consider it the most powerful tool for achieving direct contact with the unconscious. Barbara Hannah, a student of Jung's, writes:

> Although it is essential to have a human companion in whom one can confide, the actual active imagination is a very individual and even lonely undertaking. At all events, I could never do active imagination with anyone else in the room, however well I knew the person. (*Encounters with the Soul: Active Imagination* 12)

My reading confirmed some of my own insights, as, for example, the need to let the imagination flow where it will, but it also exposed me to some potential hazards in the process, particularly the possibility of being dominated by voices from the unconscious. I came to realize how easily those lacking strong ego-boundaries could be thrust into an acute state of panic or even, as Hannah cautions, a psychotic episode:

> Properly used, the method of active imagination can be of the greatest help in keeping our balance and in exploring the unknown; but misunderstood and indulged in, rather than regarded as a scientific piece of *hard work,* it can release forces in the unconscious that can overcome us. (6)

Johnson explains that it is "the conscious ego, guided by a 'sense of ethics'" that must set the limits which will protect us from instinctual forces (189). He warns that whenever a voice from the unconscious advocates behavior or attitudes that go against one's deepest values, or whenever an archetype or aspect of ourselves threatens to take over, then we are standing on dangerous ground; our response, at such a

time, must be "to answer back, to present the ethical alternative" (193). In image guidance, the presence of a guide who
is at all times cognizant of what the seeker is experiencing is
another source of protection. Though I see the guide more
as a "facilitator" of the image process than as a "director,"
there may be occasions when the guide does need to intervene if the imagery becomes destructive; so far this has not
happened during my three years of using image guidance,
but I am selective about my use of the process and always
use it in the context of prayer.

In monitoring what actually takes place in image guidance, I began noticing the attitudes and physical and emotional states of those I was working with prior to a session,
during the session and after the session. I recorded my own
affective state and the shifts that I noticed as we moved into
image guidance. I paid attention to the way images surfaced
and to my own responses to them. I asked myself how I helped
images unfold and what let me know that it was time to bring
the session to an end. I studied the ways in which I led the
seeker into a reflective state and then back to a "waking"
state. I asked the seeker what had been helpful and what had
been a hindrance. I kept track of what happened to images
between sessions and of how the seeker was able to learn from
them without my help. Gradually I developed the "methodol-
ogy" which I am now committing to paper.

In the first place I recognized the skills in myself which
made image guidance an appropriate mode of spiritual companioning for me. My highly developed intuition, my deep
respect for the wisdom of the unconscious, my ready ability
to move into poetic expression and my willingness to be
guide rather than teacher were some of the gifts at work. I
discovered that my ability to listen extended beyond hearing
to *feeling* what the seeker was saying: I was in tune with
every gesture, every change in tone or posture, every shift in

expression. As a result, the presence I communicated was that of the empathetic listener; I could enter into the image experience as participant rather than detached observer. Intuitively I knew what questions to ask and what to leave unsaid, when to be silent and when to speak, when to intervene and when to let the image accomplish its own work.

To my surprise I discovered that I was also using voice modulation—sometimes to soothe, calm and relax, sometimes to energize and prod forward, sometimes to reassure or to give courage. Because I have little consciousness of self when I am working with image guidance, it is difficult for me to explain *how* I know what to do at any given point. All I can say is that I recognize God's energy working in me just as it does in a more "conventional" spiritual companioning session. The same assumption operates in both settings: what takes place happens through the holy triangle of God, seeker and guide, and what takes place is primarily to assist the seeker understand the movement of God in his or her life.

If it is possible to identify certain qualities appropriate for those who would guide or help another through image work, so, too, there are certain qualities necessary for the one who seeks guidance. Basic to the process is mutual trust: unless the seeker implicitly trusts the guide's wisdom and motives, unless the guide can trust that the seeker is revealing "what is" without editing or holding back, then the images are going to be limited in their revelation. Trust is necessary in any spiritual companioning context, but it is even more essential in image work because there is more "at stake": the laying bare of the unconscious involves nothing less than total vulnerability. Resistance and withholding, both symptoms of mistrust, block the process.

Another essential quality for anyone who would use image guidance as a tool for spiritual growth is openness to the world of images, dreams and fantasy. Those people with whom I have used image guidance have so far all been very familiar with this world which they experience as benevolent; they have neither resisted me nor the process. Some are accustomed to meditation as a chosen way of praying; others are decidedly "mystical" in terms of their relationship with God. Many keep journals and have experimented with various ways of expressing their inner life through the arts. But regardless of prayer habits and spiritual orientation, each seeker must feel comfortable: it is never helpful to impose a technique on anyone who may be alienated by the very method which is meant to enrich.

At the same time, though I *have* used image guidance with those experiencing acute inner pain, it has only been after giving the seeker time to articulate all that is going on. Sometimes we have decided that image work must wait until the emotions have calmed down; sometimes we have decided to go ahead but to proceed "with caution." We remind ourselves that we have the freedom to stop *should* the experience surface more pain than is tolerable. So far this has never happened in my experience of image guidance, but it did occur during a session in which Liz Barry was guide; her experience underscores the importance of monitoring the process at all times.

There are directees I see regularly with whom I have never used image guidance and with whom I am unlikely to do so. These individuals are usually very insecure—so much so that their grip on life is tentative at best and any probing into the unconscious becomes an existential threat. With these directees the traditional interaction between speaker/listener is reassuring: progress is slow—often imperceptible—and there is a need to cover the same ground over and over again. As the old themes and issues replay themselves, insecurity eventually gives way to trust. The best way I can serve is by "being with": by challenging gently while supporting; by sharing my own struggles and frailty so that I don't come across as one who has "all the answers."

There are also people who are good candidates for image guidance but who have difficulties with particular issues. These issues can cause resistance, and resistance, in turn, can break down the process as in the following example. Rather than summarize the dynamics involved, I will present the seeker's evaluation sheets so that they can speak for themselves [see pp. 36–38].

The guide in this particular session had also filled out evaluation sheets, but as her comments paralleled those of the seeker, it would be redundant to reproduce them. From their experience, both people involved discovered that painful images need to be handled with care and that healing can never be rushed—either through image guidance or through any other method. This case study reflects the type of situation in which spiritual direction and psychological counseling would both be to the seeker's advantage.

Preliminaries to using image guidance involve finding a comfortable, uncluttered space, disconnecting the telephone, reducing artificial light and leaving firm instructions about "not being disturbed." Any interruption can seriously interfere with the process; the resulting frustration can be intense. Flexibility with time is also important: sometimes an hour is more than adequate; at others proper closure may involve several hours. In one session where I was seeker and Liz Barry was guide, the process took over four hours, though we didn't realize it until we had finished. This, however, is unusual and perhaps can only happen when there is a deep spiritual bonding between seeker and guide or when there is a crisis of some magnitude to be explored.

On all the occasions when I have used image guidance, I have probably spent more time establishing context than actually working with a given image. The session begins like any session of spiritual companioning: with friendly exchanges, getting comfortable, perhaps some quiet time or shared prayer. Then I listen to whatever the seeker has to say, paying particular attention to any themes or images that may surface and noting sources of joy, anxiety or pain in the narrative. Ideally the seeker has already identified relevant images before the session and has had some time to live with them; if this is not the case, then the discussion can surface some unexpected images which will also "work."

"Any old image" will *not* do; the authentic image that has something to reveal to the seeker must pre-exist before the session, even if it has not yet been claimed. Without some kind of link between seeker and image, image guidance is an empty exercise. It is only in exploring what is already there, it is only in listening to the voice that has already whispered, it is only in recognizing the picture that has already unfolded in the depths of self that the seeker can be open to revelation. The image, then, is not to be fabricated but to be identified.

If the seeker accepts a particular image as an appropriate starting point, the guide's main task is to allow full access to that image. Usually I begin by suggesting some body-loosening—uncrossing arms and legs, relaxing neck muscles, getting rid of all rigidity. Then I ask the seeker to close his or her eyes and to breathe in and out, slowly, deeply. While the seeker is doing this, I too have entered a relaxed state. I move the seeker away from present location—away from the noise of commuter trains and sirens, away from barking dogs and loud radios. I move the seeker away from present fears and anxieties, saying something like: "Breathe out all that is hurtful and distressing; breathe out all that wears you out and gets you down; breathe out all that burdens you and diminishes you . . ." The words I choose come naturally, spontaneously; they always reflect something I have learned from our earlier conversation. I tend to speak softly, slowly, but with authority; my voice often becomes deep and monotone. I continue to speak, inviting the seeker to breathe in all that is life-giving, to feel the peace of the moment, to trust the wisdom that will surface, to ask for healing and illumination. Then, when I perceive that the seeker is at rest, both physically and emotionally, I begin to evoke the image.

Exactly how this happens varies in every situation. Basically, however, I remember what the seeker has previously said about the image and use this data to help it surface in his or her consciousness. During a retreat experience, for example, a friend imaged God as the button on her shirt. My way of reawakening this image for Judy was to ask her to picture this button on her favorite shirt, to feel the tension of the fabric being held in place, to feel the strength of the button, and then, when she could feel all this, to let the image speak to her. Having led her back to the image, I sat back and waited. And then came the surprise: what had started out as a limited simile became a powerful encounter with the suffering Christ. Through a process of gentle questioning I learned that the image had leaped out of control, had jumped away from buttons and fabric, and had instead led Judy into the territory of pain where the God who comforts in turn needs to be comforted. I remember that Judy cried; I don't remember my response because this event took place at the very beginning of my work on images, several years ago. Today my intervention would be to let her cry freely; then, when the crying was "done," I would invite Judy to ask God how she could give comfort and what she was being called to do. Only when she had heard her answer would I lead her back to "waking state."

In other situations I have taken a more active role. A seminarian came up with a rather complex image: he was floating in water, playing in water, relaxed and carefree; but the water was confined by a dark tunnel which loomed over him, without beginning or end. Through careful questioning I learned that the water represented all that sustained and nurtured, especially the presence of God; it was simultaneously the womb and freedom, zest for life and union with God. The tunnel, on the other hand, represented an oppressive force that was weighing him down.

From an earlier conversation I understood that John was feeling "oppressed" by representatives of the institutional church. The superior of his order had failed to treat him as an individual; he had been too ready to expect him to "conform" to his dictates without regard for his wishes. As a result, John was sad and angry; he began to wonder whether he should leave the parish where he was assigned as deacon and questioned whether he should be ordained.

This context directed me in my approach to the water/tunnel imagery. John's ability to relax and play in the water indicated that, at the core of himself, he was at peace; what needed to shift was his response to external forces—the perceived oppression. I wanted him to experience his own power in the face of this oppression. Instead of negating the darkness of the tunnel, I invited John to image himself splashing its walls as he cavorted in the water; I encouraged him to see the mortar disintegrate and the bricks crumble. At first he laughed as he played with this image; then I saw him grow increasingly peaceful. After a few minutes of silence, I asked him to describe what had happened. He explained that he had found himself being rapidly propelled through the tunnel and jettisoned onto a beautiful beach where all was calm. This new image had given him the reassurance that he had the inner resources to deal with external stress. By being himself, by giving himself the freedom to laugh and play, by defying all that was anti-life, he would not only survive but would also bring health to those who were entrapped by institutionalism. The image not only provided its own "happy resolution," but also sustained him in days and weeks to come.

Water imagery has continued to be important for him. During one session when we had decided to sit in a quiet spot near Lake Michigan, he identified himself with a sailboat battling strong winds. There was a schooner on the lake, full sails billowing proudly, but the sailboat forged ahead, turned around, circled the schooner playfully and then set a new course. The schooner, like the tunnel, represented oppression. Captivated, both of us watched the bold antics of the little sailboat in relationship to the burdened, laborious movement of the schooner. Being able to see the images in motion allowed for fruitful dialogue and greater clarity. We enjoyed sun, wind and water, yet never strayed from our focus on the inner world.

Our last session before John's ordination reflects some of the same themes. He had mixed feelings about the approaching event: sadness at leaving the parish where he had spent most of his diaconate, uncertainty about the future, discomfort with the rigidity of community attitudes. The issues I discerned during our conversation included his need for trust, his fear of separation, his desire for the courage to move on. The image that John brought with him fitted all that he described: he saw a broken glass bird lying on the shore while a gull soared away. Almost effortlessly, John reentered the image. I invited him to soar with the gull and see where his flight would take him; I was careful to give him plenty of empty spaces, but to question him whenever his facial expressions and body language indicated moments of significance. I found myself constantly asking where the gull was going, how the gull was feeling, what the gull heard . . .

The gull flew away from the parish toward the open sea. As he approached an island, a voice said, "Come, little bird, and rest." But there were fishermen near the shore who drove him away, anxious to save their catch; near them was an abandoned wreck, blackened with algae and decay. At the next place where he hoped to settle, a group of boisterous children tried to catch him and he barely escaped with his life. Soaring and circling once more, the bird suddenly heard the voice say, "Be still and know that I am God. I am with you. I love you."

John took longer than usual to "return" from his trip. He smiled several times and moved his head around and around as though to relax after all the flying; then he opened his eyes. He looked refreshed, peaceful. When we processed the experience, we were amazed at what surfaced. In the first place John discovered that he could circle and soar and still be at peace: he didn't need to know where his first assignment was going to be; God had reassured him that even without a place to rest, he could still be "at home." In addition, John's flight had enabled him to let go of all that he was clinging to, including his present parish. The fishermen defending their catch seemed to him to represent the priests he had worked with there whom he would have to leave to their own fishing; the wreck represented an aspect of church that John rejected—he would not let himself be dragged down (or diminished) by institutional absurdity.

Much of the power of these experiences is lost in the telling, but enough remains to indicate the value of image guidance in spiritual companioning. While a more traditional session may yield rich results, image guidance plunges both seeker and guide into depths which are seldom reached through more ordinary means. Both parties involved achieve a harmony of spirit, an "at-one-ness," which goes beyond companioning; both are dramatically in touch not only with their own affectivity but also with the working of the spirit in their midst. As one seeker put it, "you get further in a shorter amount of time." This is not only because of the movement of the image *during* the session but also because of the ways it manifests itself before and afterward.

There are pitfalls to be avoided. There is always the danger that a guide would misinterpret an image, distort the context or impose his or her values on the seeker; and precisely because the possibilities are so powerful, so a negative experience could be devastating. Not only must the guide constantly "check in" with the seeker to monitor and evaluate but, even more importantly, the guide must abandon himself or herself to God's wisdom, praying through the session from beginning to end. Only then can image guidance be "of God" instead of "of the ego."

IMAGE GUIDANCE WITH A GUIDE

NAME OF GUIDE:

DATE:

1. What was the disposition of the seeker at the beginning of the session?

2. What was your own disposition?

3. What context unfolded from preliminary discussion?

4. Did the seeker bring in any specific images? If so, name them.

5. Were you able to discern any issues or needs prior to image guidance?

6. What steps did you take to prepare the seeker for image guidance?

7. How did the seeker respond to your leading?

8. What images surfaced during image guidance?

9. How did each image unfold?

10. How did you intervene and why?

11. What physical and emotional changes did you note in the seeker?

12. What physical or emotional changes did you note in yourself?

13. What prompted you to bring the image guidance to an end?

14. How did you prepare the seeker to return to a waking state?

15. How would you describe the seeker after the session?

16. How do you evaluate the experience?

IMAGE GUIDANCE WITH A GUIDE

NAME OF SEEKER:

DATE:

1. How did you feel initially?

2. What issues or needs did you bring to the session?

3. Did you bring any specific images to the session?

4. How comfortable were you when your guide readied you for image guidance?

5. Did you experience any resistance?

6. Describe how your images surfaced.

7. How did they unfold?

8. Which questions/comments were helpful?

9. Which questions/comments got in the way?

10. What changes did you note in yourself during the process?

11. What did your images reveal to you?

12. How did you feel when the session came to an end?

13. What were you able to take with you from the session?

Image Guidance Without a Guide

Praying with images is not an end in itself; it is simply a "prayer tool" which we can use in times of dryness or on other occasions when we think it might be helpful. Like any form of prayer, it is to be used judiciously: if it becomes our only way of praying, if we turn to it because it gives us a "religious high," if it blocks us from speaking what is in our heart or from listening to our God, then it is an obstacle rather than a help. On the other hand, praying with images can plunge us so immediately into the experience of God, it can connect us so thoroughly with the deepest center of self, that it is a wonderful resource. Even without a guide, we can allow images to lead us into mystery and into all the revelation that is to be found there.

All the points listed below have been covered earlier; however, they are restated here as a convenient reference, in summary form:

WHAT
1. The authentic image or useful image is not a fabrication; rather, it is "a piece of life" (Jung's term for a symbol) which speaks to us about a particular experience, event or state of being.

WHEN
2. This image can surface in our dreams, in our fantasies, in everyday circumstances. Often it seemingly comes from nowhere, without being beckoned. It can be an image which strikes us as we are reading scripture, as we are praying, as we are listening to music; it can be the image of a face we see on the street, the image of a flower which surprises us with its grace, the image of a startlingly beautiful sunset. It may be an image we want to discard because

it comes as a distraction or because it seems frivolous or even possibly obscene. What is important is that we are open to the images which come, trusting that they can speak to us in a way which is significant. Nobody else should try to impose an image on us; the true image is uniquely our own, and what it means is something we already know deep within ourselves, even if our conscious minds have not yet grasped the meaning.

WHY

3. The image comes to clarify and reveal. Very often it can help us discern what we are meant to do in a particular situation or how we are meant to "be." It can help us decide between alternatives or can illumine our relationship with God, with self, with others. Like dreams, the image is a gift to help us grow; it connects us to that small quiet voice within which we might otherwise not hear.

HOW

4. Images can only be a blessing if we choose to receive them. We need to be receptive, that is, open to the possibility of otherness, open to the fact that revelation *can* come through dreams and images. Our attitude, then, must be open-handed, though we do need to be discriminating. At times so many images may surface that we will need to evaluate which would be the most beneficial for us to work with, given the circumstances in which we find ourselves. This receptivity, this discernment, comes more easily when we are in touch with our feelings and when we take time out to "stop, pause and listen." Part of our discernment, however, involves knowing whether we are "ready" to deal with a particular image; some may be too painful for us to handle alone or even with the support of a guide.

WHO

5. We can approach our images through the process I have called "image guidance" whereby a skilled guide leads us into our image, helps us encounter it and then move beyond it, supporting us and directing us along the way. It is possible, however, for us to learn to be our own guides in this process; these are helpful steps to follow:

I. Free yourself from the desire to accomplish anything, from clock-watching and your usual routine; remind yourself that you have a right to spend time alone, with yourself, even if on the surface it may seem like a waste of time.

II. Find a quiet, uncluttered place—somewhere where prayer comes easily and where there are no risks of being disturbed. Make yourself comfortable. Remind yourself of God's presence. Ask God to speak to you through your image work.

III. Think about how your life has been going in terms of prayer, play, work, relationships. Has anything unusual happened? Are you aware of shifts in yourself? Do you experience God calling you to anything new at this time? Have you been restless or dissatisfied? Have old issues resurfaced or new issues come to the fore? Have there been any special gifts or graces that have come your way? Have you noticed any patterns in terms of your attitudes and reactions? Is there anything upsetting you? Is there any aspect of your life that you would like to change? . . .

Spend some time sifting through "where you are," perhaps reading over journal entries you may have written or remembering significant encounters or events that have taken place in recent days.

IV. When you are in touch with your own emotional "climate," see if any images come to mind which reflect what you are feeling. If nothing surfaces, don't try to force any.

V. Relax yourself through deep breathing techniques. Empty your mind of everything. "Tune out" all background noises and distractions.

VI. Concentrate all your attention on your image, if you have one, thinking of nothing else. If no image has surfaced, then wait in complete passivity, keeping your mind a blank screen until "something" appears.

VII. Become the spectator; watch your image unfold without analyzing it or judging it. Be aware of how you are feeling as it moves through different stages.

VIII. Feel free to interact with your image. Ask it what it represents and why it has come to you at this time; ask it to reveal its wisdom to you. Listen for its answer. Don't be surprised if it seems to be your own voice which is answering you. Trust the words that come, provided that they call you to life.

IX. When you feel that the image has yielded its gift to you, thank it for what you have learned. Spend some time in silent prayer, conscious of your new awareness.

X. Upon your "return," think about what the image experience has meant to you. You may want to use the suggested questions to help.

IMAGE GUIDANCE WITHOUT A GUIDE

DATE:

1. What general picture about yourself emerged before you began to work with the image?

2. How were you feeling prior to the image work?

3. Did you bring any specific image to the experience? If so, what was it and what meaning did it hold for you prior to image work?

4. Did any images surface during image work? If so, what were they?

5. How did your image unfold?

6. What physical or emotional changes did you note in yourself as your image unfolded?

7. Were you able to interact verbally with your image? If so, what questions do you remember asking?

8. Did your image speak to you in any way?

9. Did your image reveal anything to you in a non-verbal way?

10. Were you conscious of God's presence during the experience?

11. What prompted you to bring the experience to an end?

12. What physical or emotional changes did you note in yourself?

13. How do you evaluate the experience?

14. What have you learned, in terms of technique, that you will be able to use the next time you pray with images?

Image Guidance in a Small Group Context

Since image guidance involves the exploration of the unique, spontaneous image as it occurs in the consciousness of an individual, to speak of image guidance as a group experience seems like a contradiction in terms. I have, however, used a blend of guided imagery and the image guidance method in small retreat groups and workshops; my strategy is to do a minimal amount of leading and then to leave the resolution of the experience "open ended." Group processing then provides participants with suggestions for further explorations on their own.

The group experience can take a variety of forms. A guided meditation, for example, takes participants on a similiar journey—perhaps on a descent into their inner depths, perhaps on a quest to remove those rocks and boulders which make God inaccessible, perhaps on a heroic mission to encounter some dragon or demon. An audio-visual experience involving slides and music can also move the group along a similar experiential path, before leaving them to their own image-making faculties. Meditating on a particular object—a battered hat or a worn teddy bear—can also set a group experience in motion, as can sharing a particular food or participating in a dance. In the following example I use a scripture reflection as starting point, but the processing which follows is typical of other "group experiences."

Scripture Reflection: Jn 4:5–42

> Deep, deep beneath all the stones and rubble, deep, deep beneath all the dry sands and all the arid ground is a secret well; and in that well, deep within the very depths of ourselves, you are hiding, God—right in the heart of that very place

where we would least expect to find you. All that separates you from us are our own particular pebbles, stones and boulders; we bury you under the weight of our incompleteness—under our fears, our attachments, our addictions, our compulsions, our obsessions, our frailty. And because we do not have eyes to see or ears to hear, because we have closed ourselves off from our dreams and from our feelings, because we insist on following *our* star instead of yours, God, we look for you outside ourselves. We think that cathedrals and churches hold your mystery; we escape to mountains and wilderness places, hoping to find you there. And you laugh sadly, shaking your head at our folly, wondering if we will ever learn . . .

The truth of the matter is that there is nothing more important than this well of ours. Nothing we do, nothing we achieve, nothing we desire is more important than this wellspring of life—your presence within us. But we do not happen upon it by accident, nor do we discover it simply by demanding water. Rather, we must first recognize that you alone can satisfy our thirst; we must first acknowledge that it is our own sinfulness that blocks us from receiving the living water you offer us. We must fashion for ourselves buckets of humility and trust; and then, with your help, we can lower them, slowly, reverently, into the depths where you reside . . .

I read this scripture reflection without commentary. Then, when I had finished, I turned off the lights and invited the group to enter the silence and to see what images would surface. Ten minutes later, I turned the lights back on so that we could process what had "happened." My function was to listen, to summarize and then to give suggestions for future individual work. The three following "case studies" will demonstrate the variety of experiences which the reflection generated:

Subject 1:

"As I lowered my bucket, I noticed that it was made of beautiful green glass—Tiffany glass with floral designs on the sides. The well was narrow and I was concerned that the bucket would break in the descent. However, the deeper the bucket went, the more beautiful it became. It was studded with brilliant jewels which radiated light through the dark water. And the deeper the bucket went, the clearer the water became—it was clear blue and effervescent. Then I noticed that the bucket and the water became one—it was as though the glass dissolved into the water, leaving only the black chains which had supported the bucket . . ."

Summary:

"So you really concentrated on fashioning a bucket of humility and trust?"

"Yes."

"And the experience brought unexpected richness, leading to what we could call a 'unitive experience' of God's presence?"

"Yes."

"How did you feel when the experience ended?"

"I wanted it to go on—I felt cheated because I felt so close to God, so much in touch with myself."

Suggestion:

"Take the image of the glass bucket to prayer. Picture the well in all its depth and picture yourself as the bucket, descending into the deepest place where God resides. Ask God to guide you in this descent and to take you as deep as you are meant to go at this present time."

Subject 2:

"My imagery took me far away from the well and the bucket. I saw a little girl, dressed in white, who was struggling to break free of her bindings. Finally, she was able to get away from whatever was imprisoning her and to run free. She was happy, very much alive—and I knew I was that little girl."

Summary:

"So when you thought of the water, freedom came to mind, as well as recovering something that you may have lost in childhood?"

"Yes. I was so surprised to see the little girl—I asked her to stay with me when you turned the lights on. She has been lost for years—ever since I was abused by my father. I don't want to lose her again."

Suggestion:

"Make that little girl your companion. Ask her why she was lost, how she felt, how she feels now; ask her how you can make her a part of your life again; take her to prayer so that both of you can find healing. Ask God to restore any part of you that may have dried up and died during childhood."

Subject 3:

"I didn't get to the well or to the bucket—instead, I was trying to *dig* the well. Even though I had a shovel, there was a great deal of work to do. I dug and dug but there was no water in sight . . ."

Summary:

"You sound sad."

"Yes, I have a great sense of loss—a feeling that I'm putting my energy in the wrong places and missing out on something very important."

"Can you name this more specifically?"

"Yes. I feel I've neglected my inner life—that somehow I haven't learned how to find a place for God in my busy schedule. I feel like such a novice at prayer . . ."

Suggestion:

"Ask Jesus to help you with the digging. Invite him to pick up the shovel and help you break the ground; tell him that you cannot do it alone. Then, when you can see the water, ask him to help you fashion a bucket so that you can lower it into the rich, rich waters below."

NAME OF SEEKER: Mary S.

NAME OF GUIDE: Liz B.

DATE: 2/8/91

1. How did you feel initially?
I was excited about going into the session but a bit appre-
hensive. I knew what image I needed to work with but
did not realize the emotional undercurrents would be so
intense.

2. What issues/needs did you bring to the session?
I brought a strong need to communicate with my child
within.

3. Did you bring any specific images to the session?
The image I have carried with me for many years is a
little girl around five years old. Her hair is shoulder
length, tangled and messy. Her dress is weather-beaten
and her little boots are quite old. She sits by herself in the
corner of the room on the floor. Her eyes are blue.

4. How comfortable were you when your guide read-
ied you for image guidance?
The process felt very natural. I do meditation on my
own, so the breathing and clearing my mind were familiar. Liz's voice is soothing and her presence was comfortable to be around.

5. Did you experience any resistance?
Not at first—not until I had moved into the image.

6. Describe how your images surfaced.

On going into my center, the child was right there. There was no probing her out of a corner. She was right there. As I stood in the center of my being with my child standing right in front of me, the area around us was void of all things.

7. How did they unfold?

Liz suggested that I go up to the child and hug her, but I couldn't. The child looked at me, and without moving her mouth she spoke to me from her heart. Her words were, "Why can't you hug me?" I had no words to give her because I was conscious of having an audience— and there was too much pain. I kept on remembering how she had been neglected and put down. I thought about how weird everyone thought she was—some kind of freak—and how wonderful it was when Dad would come home because then Mom would stop beating her. I remembered how she would defend herself by hyperventilating—that scared her Mom and stopped the beatings, but her sister would get it more. And the little girl hated her sister for being so weak and for not knowing how to run away. And she was so lonely because she had no friends and her sister blamed her for her mother's anger.

8. Which questions/comments were helpful?

The questions about what the child looked like and the direction to give the child a hug—that let me know how much I was hurting.

9. Which questions/comments got in the way?

The hug direction—it was helpful but it also broke my

concentration. I *couldn't* hug the child—I wanted to, but something in me wanted her to go away. I wanted to forget about her. I opened my eyes and told Liz I had had enough.

10. What changes did you note in yourself during the process?

My body seemed very large—as though I was not contained within my bodily frame. I felt as though my body was moving without my controlling the movement. It was all so peaceful—I felt beautiful inside.

11. What did your images reveal to you?

My child gave me the sense that she knew I would continue working at this relationship until I could embrace her with love. She just knew this and would wait.

12. How did you feel when the session came to an end?

Beautiful and embarrassed. My body tingled with beauty and yet I was embarrassed that I had not been able to stay with the image. But I left with a yearning for more—I felt the need to do some processing on my own before I could return.

2
Myths and Symbols

In using image guidance in spiritual direction, I have come to expect that the images which present themselves will very likely be archetypal in nature and that as they unfold they may provide variations of mythical themes. My task, as I have come to understand it, is to be aware of any similarities to archetypes and mythical motifs with which I am familiar, while keeping my focus on the experience at hand. While my background in myths often enriches my skill at "being with" a seeker, I must listen to every story as though I am hearing it for the first time and not too readily assume that I am hearing yet another version of the quest for the Holy Grail. At the same time, my awareness of mythical and archetypal "connections" does help me to understand dimensions of seekers' journeys which would otherwise be inaccessible to me; this understanding can direct me in the kinds of questions I pose, in the way I assist the seeker to return to "ordinary" consciousness, and also in my analysis of "what was going on" during a particular session. My "mythical consciousness," then, does shape my responses and is perhaps largely responsible for the "intuitive knowing" I bring to image guidance.

The world of dreams and myths has always fascinated

me. As a child I was captivated by stories of heroes performing impossible feats at great personal risk. There were dragon slayers, riddle solvers and cunning rescuers; there were princesses to be saved, mazes to be unraveled and wastelands to redeem; there were tedious tasks and noble battles, victory and glorious death. I read of Perseus and Hercules, of Odysseus and Hector, of Pandora and Eve . . . I wept with them and gloried with them, dreamed about them and placed myself in my dreams, often as redeeming hero. Whether they succeeded or failed, these heroes of mine stretched the limits of what it meant to be human: they refused to accept "no" as an answer; rather, they lived life on their terms, often in defiance of the gods. They chose curiosity and adventure over obedience; they preferred uncertainty to predictability and safety. And, whatever the outcome of their choices, they left me with the conviction that life was rich and wonderful.

It was through these dream myths that I first became acquainted with the world of the unconscious. Images of keys and golden doors, of mermaids and wise women, of rescuers and gift givers, soon became part of my fantasy world. I drew pictures and acted out scenarios, I modeled figures of clay and read and reread fairy tales. Images of silver chalices and golden fleeces, of persuasive serpents and wrathful angels, of dangerous sirens and benevolent beggars soon took on a reality that went beyond the literary. These images returned over and over again, schooling me, forming me, empowering me in ways I did not understand. They helped me to break free from stereotypes of time, class and culture and to dare to imagine an alternative future: I did not have to follow established patterns; rather, I could create my own path as I walked along it, sometimes planning ahead, sometimes surprising myself, and sometimes suffering for it.

"Courage," "authenticity," and "integrity" became ideals long before I was old enough to know what the words meant.

Years later, as I became familiar with the works of Carl Jung, Mircea Eliade and Joseph Campbell, I began to understand the power of archetypal imagery in both dreams and myths. Though my early experiences with images—some of them surfaced when I was barely five—had seemed uniquely my own, yet they belonged to the collective unconscious: they were my legacy from those who had walked before me; at the same time, they connected me with my contemporaries of every race and creed. Though they seemed private— and I kept them hidden out of embarrassment—they were common; though they held unique meaning for me as an individual, they held general meaning which others could recognize, if they had the necessary skills to do so.

It was not only in myth but in the simple beauty of things of the earth that I discovered images of the God I am still seeking. I was much influenced by Malta, the Mediterranean island where I spent most of my childhood. As I danced along the seashore, gathering shells and pebbles, as I ran through fields, breaking off bits of cauliflower heads and sucking on the sweet stems of yellow wildflowers, as I marveled at the assortment of lizards and geckos that darted under the grape vine or up the trunk of the gnarled fig tree, I learned to know a God who delighted in life, in all things bright and beautiful, all creatures great and small—myself included.

I found God in the clumps of wild thyme and the caper bushes which cascaded over the rugged cliffs, hundreds of feet above sea level. I found God in the poinsettia which splashed red, ten feet high, against the garden wall, weaving a rich tapestry against white stone. I found God in my perch in the ancient carob tree at the fork of the dusty country road which ran alongside my parents' five hundred year old house. God was in the citrus groves and flowering shrubs, in the geranium bushes and terraced fields, in fossilized shells and sharks' teeth embedded in rock; God was in the clods of red earth and in the crude cart tracks, millennia old, which baffled peasants and archaeologists alike. God was in the mystery and in the beauty, in the vastness and in the details, but, most especially, in the uniqueness of each living thing.

This God who filled and transcended creation was also to be found in water. As a child I knew nothing of the symbolic significance of water—that it represents the feminine depths associated with the descent into the unconscious, that it embodies the stillness that is before birth, that it connotes the healing forces which support and sustain life. Rather, I was lured by water, captivated by it, mesmerized by its depths. I was barely six when I tried walking on water in response to a dare. The scene was Geneva, Switzerland; the water was Lac Leman. Then I didn't know that flesh is heavier than air, more solid than water. I thought it was a matter of will, of placing one foot before the other and watching my reflection in the lake below. I was surprised when I sank—surprised, too, by the screams rising above water as I splashed, swallowed, then surrendered to the current. My musings about sharks, crabs and the distant *jet d'eau* were shattered by the abruptness of a lame man's cane; his words of urgency sounded through the water like a message from another world and I clung to his staff . . .

This episode left me afraid of anything deeper than the bathtub. Not until several years later did I decide that if I used a mask, snorkel and flippers, I could brave the Mediterranean and discover a world of incredible beauty and color. I delighted in the darting fish, in the hermit crabs scuttling along the sandy seabed, in the starfish and anemones which seemed so delicate, in the sea urchins clinging to craggy rocks. What I enjoyed the most, however, was the feeling of absolute freedom, of moving in another dimension, of being one with the water and feeling literally surrounded by otherness. God was present; swimming was prayer.

It was not only my underwater experiences that drew me to the Mediterranean. I delighted in the sea in all its moods—in lashing winds and tempestuous waves; in the black, white-crested sea of night and the surging gray of stormy days; in the stillness of deep turquoise and in the oily roll of harbor waves. The sea stilled me, filled me with awe and wonder, made me feel its power. And as I gazed at fiery red sunsets at the point where sea met sky, I felt the presence of God the creator.

Mystery was also present in the neolithic temples scattered all over the island. As a teenager, I explored the womb-like clusters of stone, older than Stonehenge and more impressive. I felt small next to the monoliths; I felt wonder as I looked at the spiral-decorated stone altars within cultic chambers. There was a simplicity in those temples which spoke more deeply to my spirit than any of the gaudy baroque churches, but there was also a power. Perhaps it was the massive scale of the temples which filled me with awe. Perhaps I was dimly aware of the connection between death and life, womb and tomb, emptiness and fullness. Here, after all, the feminine principle predominated: life issued from the womb of the goddess; death was a return to that womb where one could be reborn. Perhaps I felt drawn to that image of inspiration, intuition and receptivity—"the sleeping lady"; crudely carved with exaggerated breasts and hips as she reclines on a four-legged couch, the figurine is thought to represent a priestess receiving divine intelligence in her dreams. The temples, then, spoke to my unconscious in deep and significant ways.

Myths, dreams, and images of earth, water and temple exerted a profound influence over me, shaping my spirituality, putting me in touch with hidden depths within myself. They intensified both my love of beauty and my sense of wonder, heightening my receptivity to things mysterious. As an adult they drew me toward interests in literature and scripture, archaeology and liturgy; they sparked in me the strong desire to express all that I saw and heard, touched and tasted. Before long, I was writing poetry—exploring biblical and mythical motifs, drawing on images from the Maltese landscape, creating a surreal world of dream-like intensity. And the words simply flowed from the unconscious, page after page, book after book, as though they had pre-existed and were simply waiting for me to discover them . . .

Somewhat tentatively I began to experiment with images in the classroom. Instead of simply encouraging clinical analysis of the images which surfaced, I encouraged students to examine their gut responses instead. "How does this make you feel?" "What associations does this hold for you?" "What doors does this image open for you?"—these became typical questions. I wanted my students to enter into the sensory world offered by each image, to experience it to the fullest degree possible and to react—perhaps orally, perhaps in written form, perhaps in art, music or dance. The main challenge involved knowing the group and being aware of thresholds of resistance—not everyone wants to move at the same pace or is capable of doing so; moreover, not everyone is willing to "go public" with what is essentially private.

In creative writing classes, I began to provide a "seed-bed" for images—perhaps a short story, or a photograph, or a piece of music or an artifact. Then, after 10–15 minutes of reflective silence, we would discuss what we saw, heard and felt in that silence; only then would we attempt to write our responses in poetry or prose. One successful exercise involved asking students to bring in their baby pictures so that they could dialogue with the child they saw reflected there and with their memories of that child. On another occasion, I read the group Shel Silverstein's *The Missing Piece;* this generated images of what it means to be "complete" or "incomplete," as well as images of seeking, finding and willingly surrendering. Since everyone shared a common starting point, we had a context for understanding the images which surfaced, however varied they happened to be. Though we spent time critiquing the quality of the writing, our main focus was self-discovery and the guidance offered by the images themselves.

In graduate classes on myth, ritual and symbol, I encouraged students to understand the function of images in their own experience. As we covered such topics as archetypes and private symbols, language as symbolic action, myths of creation and fall, myths of death and resurrection, Christian signs and symbols and revitalizing the ecclesial imagination, we recorded the impact that related images held for each of us. One student who had been struck by Mircea Eliade's emphasis on "remembering" as sacred activity put together photographs and accompanying meditations which traced her spiritual roots. Another student who had recently lost her mother explored motifs of death and resurrection in her own life through original poetry. Yet another produced a series of plaster hands in varying positions (bound, for example, like those of a prisoner) as a way of providing contemporary symbols of oppression. And another went on a vision quest, soliciting the help of a lifeguard who rowed her out onto Lake Michigan where she surrendered emblems of a former way of life to the deep . . .

During our time together, we learned from the texts we studied but even more especially from the collective wisdom of the class. I began to realize even more fully the profound impact myths could have on people's lives and saw, in action, the transformative energy that can be released in those who are in touch with their unique symbol systems. From our class process, I learned the meaning of Jung's assertion that in former times, people "did not reflect upon their symbols; they lived them and were unconsciously animated by their meaning" (69). Over and over again, I saw students recognizing pieces of their own lives—pieces of themselves, in fact—in the ancient stories we retold. Over and over again, I saw them discovering in themselves archetypal patterns of behavior. Through such books as Robert Johnson's *He, She* and *We,* Carol Pearson's *The Hero Within,* and Gerald Slusser's *From Jung to Jesus,* we were able to name the psychological realities that were operative in our own lives and to understand them from the vantage point of myth. Sometimes, these epiphany moments would be honored with rituals (as in the case of the "vision quest" mentioned above); at others, they would be followed by dramatic decisions, as for example, to change jobs or end a destructive relationship. In *The Mythic Imagination,* Stephen Larsen points out the paradox inherent in the term "personal mythology":

> Myths are by nature transpersonal—beyond individuals—and their elements are universal themes. How, then, can they be 'personal'? Whenever any of us becomes a hero, a dragon, a princess, or any of the other dramatis personae of the mythological world, we are dissolved in an archetype—an identity larger than ourselves. Our personal uniqueness perishes as we enter an eternal role. And yet it is only through entering this paradoxical zone that we truly find our individuality. (3)

This reflects precisely what happened in our classroom: by penetrating mythical quests of a universal nature, we received deeper insights into our own journeying.

I have found it useful at times to deliberately introduce a mythological framework into counseling contexts. If those undergoing painful experiences can reflect on their lives from the vantage point of the heroic quest, how much easier it is to move beyond the pain and to channel one's energies into positive action! If, for example, one can see in situations of dissatisfaction or loss a call to high adventure, then limiting events can become bearable. If one can imagine that the blocks or obstacles lying ahead are dragons guarding the threshold of adventure, then the task of overcoming them is ennobling. If one has to lean upon helpers to survive, then the knowledge that this is a temporary phase of the heroic quest provides the assurance that there will be a time when independence will be a possibility. And if the road of trials is seemingly without end, then to know that one is walking the path to increased consciousness at least offers a little comfort where perhaps there would be none.

One woman—a stranger in crisis—found her way to my door. She had recently lost her job after discovering a situation of grave injustice which she had reported to her supervisor. Having tried the legal avenues available, she realized there was little—if anything—she could do to regain her position. Meanwhile, she had had to drop out of her Master's program because she could no longer afford tuition and was having a difficult time supporting herself and her young child. I could not "fix things" for her, but in our brief conversation I was able to redirect her through the language of myth. "How can you use this situation to empower you?" I asked. "What have you learned that will make a difference to your future? How can you turn these trials around so that you can gain wisdom? In what ways can this experience lead you to an heroic quest? What gifts can you receive from this quest that will benefit others?"

As she listened, I saw her become more animated, more

hopeful; the look of defeat began to disappear. Somewhat shyly she began to tell me of a dream she had of becoming an advocate for the poor—particularly for blacks in urban settings. Perhaps losing her job was the catalyst that would make her act upon this dream . . . Perhaps losing her job would teach her how to protect herself in similar situations . . . Perhaps her money struggles would give her greater empathy for those who experienced poverty on a regular basis . . .

Several weeks later, I received a card depicting a hare—symbol of transformation/resurrection; in it she thanked me for helping her understand the journey she needed to take . . .

In image guidance, mythical elements surface naturally, without any prompting from the guide. In the following case study, I analyze my own reactions to them as they unfold:

Bob wanted to work on his desire for awareness. He had no specific image, so I invited him to close his eyes, but to be aware of his external surroundings—particularly of the storm raging outside. I also instructed him to be conscious of his body—the weight of his hands on his thighs, the straightness of his spine, the position of his feet. I encouraged him to listen to his breathing and to be aware of his heartbeat . . .

The image that came to him was of the darkness and vastness of outer space; he could see bent rays of light which represented consciousness for him. From his description I had the feeling that he was moving into a "cosmic" kind of experience. I asked him how he felt. He was afraid and didn't want to take the first step, even though he knew he was on the threshold of some great and wonderful adventure. He wanted to go forward but lacked courage. Remembering the role of "helper" in fables and myths, I asked Bob if there was anyone he knew who had already taken this step. "Jane," he said. "She's been writing poetry for ten years and has probed inward extensively." I knew that while

Bob had explored the collective unconscious and was intent upon inner journeying, he was afraid of exploring his personal unconscious. I instructed him to ask Jane to hold his hand as he stepped across the threshold . . .

Mythologically speaking, darkness is both benign and harmful, friend and enemy. We go into the darkness to be knit together (as in the womb) or to discover new inner depths (Joseph in the well) or to be purged of ego-attachments (Jonah in the belly of the great fish); darkness, however, can also unleash chaos and inhuman forces—as, for example, the dark contents of Pandora's box. I was unconcerned about Bob stepping out into the darkness because it was a positive energy that was drawing him; moreover, the bent rays of light which had symbolized consciousness for him were also a part of the waiting experience and actually imaged what he hoped to attain.

Tightly gripping Jane's hand, Bob stepped into the darkness, only to discover that his head had come off. In myths, fables and accounts of shamanic vision quests, dismemberment of one form or another is the prelude to higher consciousness: to lose one's head may be an indication that other aspects of self need to be developed. Without commenting, I listened as Bob described his journey:

"I'm not in pain—in fact, I don't really miss my head. The darkness holds me up, supports me. I hesitate, not wanting to go any deeper into the darkness, and suddenly I can see a bubble of light—it is vast, as vast as the darkness. There's a fairy godmotherly sort who tells me I can go as deeply into the light as I desire . . ."

The presence of the immense light bubble informed me that Bob was indeed about to explore his own unconscious depths and that the experience would be a positive one. By bringing to the light that which had previously been repressed, he would find the power and strength for further inward quests. The fairy godmother, like wisdom figures in various mythical or literary traditions, was a voice to be trusted. Her invitation allowed Bob to choose how far he went while knowing that the journey would be safe.

"I begin walking into the bubble. Ahead, there are beautiful fields and woods—I feel as though I have been here before. It seems a waste of time, going over the same ground. Now a wolf enters the picture and accompanies me into a dark wood. There are unknown terrors here; the bottom branches of the trees are missing and I wonder what has happened to them. There doesn't seem to be a path, either. We seem to be wandering around aimlessly. The territory seems very, very old. I feel a deep chilling fear as I see an enormous Cyclops Bug—I feel panic. I don't want to go on . . ."

Seeing the terror in Bob's face, I instructed him to ask the wolf what he should do. Without my prompting, it was possible that he would have remained trapped in the wood. My previous work with Bob had made me familiar with his tendency to get stuck in negative memories and his resistance to breaking free from the chains of the past. I trusted that the wolf, like many woodland animals, would be another wisdom figure; it did not seem to have a sinister aspect.

"The wolf says I should walk straight ahead without stopping and that the Cyclops Bug can't harm me. He said I've spent long enough in this wood. But I don't have the energy to go on . . . Now there's a knight, urging me to go forward . . ."

Again I intervened. "Bob, listen to the knight. You need to steel yourself for the journey. Get up and walk. Leave the dark wood behind you and know that a gift lies ahead . . ."

In the distance, Bob could see what looked like an Emerald City; it glittered enticingly, and he found himself motivated to investigate. He hurried onward, leaving the darkness of the wood behind him, but when he drew close to the city, the face of the stereotypical angry God with a white flowing beard appeared. Bob stopped in his tracks. I instructed him to ask the God why he was angry. The dialogue went something like this:

> "God, why are you angry?"
> "Because you won't go on your journey—you keep putting it off."
> "What should I do, God?"
> "Spend some time in the city."

Bob did as he had been instructed. In the city, he felt energized, alive, at peace. The image of God became tranquil—his face grew as calm as a Buddha's; his eyes closed; he was no longer angry. Noting that Bob looked very much like the God he had described, I invited him to find a quiet spot within the city and to spend some time in contemplation there. Then, when he was ready, he could rejoin me in my office. He remained in what I would describe as a "blissful state" for about five minutes before returning to ordinary consciousness. During our processing of the experience, I reminded him that he could return to the Emerald City whenever he wanted and that he would find within it those inner gifts which so often eluded him.

TO:	Liz Vanek
FROM:	Bob
DATE:	March 5, 1991
RE:	Reflections on Image Guidance

I have found image guidance to be most helpful. At times the sessions are trying; they certainly involve work. And, initially, they were even disturbing. One early session, in which I worked with a powerful dream image involving a dangerous cliff overlooking the sea, was followed by a couple of days feeling "out of sorts." In that session the dream image led to my encounter as a young boy with a somewhat tired, once-wounded knight. I was angry with him, believing he was in part to blame for my condition. Though I attempted to "resolve" my relationship with him, I was left still angry, and also sad.

Despite these uncomfortable feelings, I knew that these images were "alive," meaningful, and powerful, and that they shouldn't be ignored.

Still, after a couple of sessions, I was somewhat reluctant to continue, wondering, "Do I need this aggravation?" I'm thankful I did continue.

One thing I have learned is that image guidance affords one the opportunity for resolution of issues related to images that resonate for us. In one session I confronted a negative dream experience in which I felt rejected by several family members. They'd been unwilling to cooperate with my wish to photograph the group. In the session I simply asked each member why this was a problem. I got answers. Some agreed they were being inconsiderate; others let me know of their underlying feelings: they didn't approve of the way I led my life. Once again, something uncomfortable. But I was able to dialogue with these people, explaining my life choices, essentially defending myself. I felt a greater respect for myself, and they did, too. While one of them still seemed reluctant to concede very much, at least I showed resolve. In the dream I had merely walked away carrying a sense of rejection.

Image guidance has taught me to have more confidence in the process of "inner dialogue" with images, even to the point where I now rather easily verbalize aloud my dialogues during sessions, for these dialogues are in ways "more real" than are usual conversations. They're a powerful tool for carrying images further, for seeing what's "behind" or "within" images. Only through dialoguing was I able to realize what motivated my family members as they refused to cooperate.

I even dialogued in one session with an inanimate object, a stone which blocked my path. It let me know that it stood for everything within that blocks me from further growth, the barriers of fear and self-doubt I place in front of me.

As I attempted to get around it, it grew larger. But instead of resigning myself to going no further, I resolved to enter it—and a door was there for me. Once inside, I discovered a primitive temple, a place of great peace and centeredness. I drew a deer on its wall—a creative act. A simple dialogue in fact opened a door to a wonderful place, which I knew to be *my* temple. So while there may be barriers within me, there also exist great possibilities.

This is what image guidance provides: the opportunity to go much further with an image. It does that because it serves as a bridge between the conscious and the unconscious minds. And though it is guided, it is a personal journey. No one dictates what one is to see. It's a matter of personal discovery. And the unconscious is rich in possibilities:

knights, temples, insights about people. One session led me to an encounter with a princess trapped in a gloomy castle controlled by a witch, but I was able to save the princess by finding her a glorious castle. The issue in that session was my difficulty believing I could write (the witch). What I experienced was the glorious exercise of my imagination (the castle).

These images still resonate. A session doesn't end; it enhances a process begun by the image itself. I might return to my knight, or my princess, or my temple, and further the experience. Perhaps a dream will do that for me. In my session involving the temple, I left the temple through a different door, in the back, and, after giving thanks to the temple, continued down a path.

3
Image Guidance as a Means of Understanding One's Relationship with God

One of the major benefits of image guidance is that it allows us to move beyond outgrown images and to experience relationship with God in ways that are fresh and meaningful. If our images of mystery remain static, then, the chances are, so does our spiritual life. The challenge is to perceive when our images are shifting and why they need to shift. Without this awareness we lose the potential for growth and transformation: we stay "stuck" in what was appropriate for us in the past.

Let us journey back for a moment to ancient Babylon. There the gods were carved of wood, plated in silver and gold, and sumptuously dressed in rich fabrics and precious jewelry. These images stood on pedestals in the sanctuary. Endowed with life through sacred rituals, they were washed, dressed, and fed breakfast, lunch and dinner. Sometimes they were taken on divine peregrinations for the benefit of the people; sometimes they were entertained with music, wrestling, acrobatics and sword-swallowing. "If someone does not rub off the tarnish, these gods will not do much shining on their own," Jeremiah warned those about to be led captive into Babylon (Baruch 6). We may smile when we remember the images of God held by earlier civilizations; however, we should not too readily pride ourselves on our sophistication. Just as earlier peoples tried to come to an understanding of God, so do we; and just as the concept of God evolved over millennia, so too our own images of God evolve in our individual lifetimes.

There is a direct correlation between how we view God and our experience of God. The more limited our images, the more limited our experience; conversely, the more expansive our images, the more expansive our experience. As children we may have viewed God as a benevolent old man, a cartoon Santa Claus who would grant any whim provided we were "good"; we may have viewed God's Son as the smiling Infant whose birthday offered an occasion for feasting and presents. It does not take much imagination to realize that while these images may "work" for a pre-schooler, they hardly advance an adult along the path of faith. Just as we outgrow clothes as our bodies change, so too we outgrow images and need to move beyond them. Russian nesting dolls provide a colorful analogy: theoretically each doll could fit inside another larger doll ad infinitum; it is not that the tiniest doll is insignificant, but the reality it represents gives way to a larger reality which actually grows out of it. The tiniest of dolls, for example, could represent a God who is to be feared and placated if possible. The doll one size up could represent a God upon whose good will all basic needs depend. The next largest doll could stand for a God who takes an interest in individuals . . . Each image mirrors an aspect of God that is important for us to see at a particular stage of our spiritual development; no single image could ever convey more than a fraction of the reality.

Expanding an image is more difficult than finding clothes to fit a new body shape or playing with nesting dolls. Because of our love of security, our image of God can become idolatrous: we cling so closely to the image that we don't allow God to be anything else for us. We define God in terms that seem safe and predictable, respectable and "orthodox." We try to control God by not allowing God to be Godself. For example, we cling to the baby in the cradle because he is less dangerous than an adult Christ who might call us to frightening uncertainties; that baby allows us to feel warm and snug inside whereas an adult Jesus may leave us feeling pulled, tugged and challenged. Or we may nail Jesus firmly to the cross and leave him there because it is easier to weep over a crucified God than to embrace a resurrected Jesus who just might send us to the ends of the earth with a mandate to proclaim the gospel to all creation. Then, again, we may see God so firmly as "Father" that we never stop to think that God has motherly aspects too, or that we may possibly be imposing on God some of our own negative feelings about our biological parents.

The problem with clutching an outgrown image is that we stunt our ability to pray: image dictates attitude and attitude dictates prayer experience. Someone who sees God primarily as "judge" will most likely fear God and pay scrupulous attention to rules and commandments; that person will tend to pray out of obligation and to rely on what I will call "pre-fabricated" prayer instead of spontaneous prayer or the silent prayer of the heart. In contrast, the one who sees God primarily as "creator" tends to experience wonder, awe and a sense of God's "otherness"; prayer is very often rooted in gratitude. Then, again, someone who sees God as "liberator" will be filled with longing for the reign of God and will boldly plead and demand on behalf of the suffering world, insisting that God act here and now and not in some distant future time. Similarly, the one who sees God as "be-loved" will yearn for the burning presence of God; prayer is union, contemplative wonder, silence . . .

Changing images is not a matter of will but a matter of openness. We do not select images from a range of choices, cafeteria style; instead, we learn to recognize when images are not working and wait for new ones to surface in our day-to-day waking and dreaming, in our reading of scripture. Mary, an incest survivor, was terrified of a God who was out to "zap" her; because of her openness, in less than a year she was able to move beyond this image to the image of a broken-hearted God who had been with her in all her pain and wanted only her happiness. David, a homosexual, has projected onto God all the hostility and judgmentalism he experiences from the establishment; until he opens himself to the possibility of alternative images, he is going to remain trapped in a fear-based relationship with God. Ted, a sexually-active Catholic priest, will continue to have problems with celibacy until he finds a God who, hungry for his love, is willing to embrace him . . .

Through image guidance we can understand which im-ages are operative for us. While on our own we may notice the images of God which surface most frequently, with the help of a guide we can enter into those deep places within and perhaps find more than we bargained for. Anne, for example, had experienced God's seeming absence for sev-eral months. There were difficulties in her private life, ten-sions at work and a sense of loss over opportunities for minis-try. In the past she had usually been able to find consolation in prayer; now, nothing "worked." She was exhausted, over-whelmed and bereft of images; she needed to know where God was in the midst of this pain.

I invited her to imagine herself in a garden of contempla-tion and to see what would unfold. Gradually, she described the garden of her childhood, a European garden filled with roses, geraniums and citrus trees. She saw herself on the garden swing, flying high, high, high, until she could see over the ten foot wall. She saw herself, again as a child, sitting by the goldfish pond, watching the terrapins that lived there. She saw herself climbing on a ladder to reach heavy bunches of grapes which trailed from an archway and to pluck the figs from a five hundred year old tree. She saw her parents and her grandparents, her sisters, her aunts and uncles, her cousins and friends—and she felt secure. In fact, she didn't want to move.

Then a shift happened. A thick forest came into view and, through the trees, Anne could see a light, faint at first, but then bright and inviting. She tried to resist, but the light became more and more insistent, beckoning her, in spite of her desire to stay rooted to her childhood garden. Slowly, reluctantly, she found herself leaving her garden and walking toward the light; behind her, a door slammed shut, blocking her return. Feeling bereaved, she continued to walk forward into brighter intensity still. The light was pure, blinding . . .

Then another garden surfaced—one straight out of a Monet canvas depicting water lilies. The water was purple-blue, dotted with patches of green and white lily pads. There were two benches close to the pond, but Anne saw herself ignoring them and walking into the water, merging with the water until there was no distinction between her and the reality Monet had evoked. The tears streamed down her face . . .

This imagery put Anne in touch with powerful emotions: grief, sense of loss and hunger for union with God. She came out of the experience understanding the depth of her pain but she also felt a sense of healing. The childhood garden impressed upon her her desire to stay where it was safe, to be left alone, without any challenges or pressures. At the same time, the light which drew her from the garden seemed to represent God's invitation to her to move on and beyond where she was at present. She experienced this light as a pledge of presence, even if she felt nothing but sadness. The closer she drew to the light, the brighter it became and the stronger she grew. She understood that her survival meant walking forward, toward the beauty of the water lily pond: here God was not to be contemplated from a distance; rather, she was to plunge into the depths of God, into the depths of all that is life-giving and mysterious. She was no longer afraid.

In another session, image guidance helped Anne to understand her relationship with God even more clearly and to articulate what she learned. She brought with her the image of a woman seated at the foot of the cross, gazing up at the white cloth draped over the horizontal bar. This image had reoccurred several times in prayer and she was eager to explore it further. I led her through the usual relaxation exercises, inviting her to breathe in the warmth, light and fire of the love energy that filled her, and to breathe out anything that caused her distress. When she had reentered her prayer image, I asked her to concentrate on what she saw. Gradually she spoke of how she and the cloth were one, and that she understood the image to represent her being in union with God. While she was still in the image, I asked her whether this union were spousal; her response was that spousal love did not adequately communicate her experience of union—that "two in one flesh" was a different reality than being so at-one with God that there was no longer any distinction between subject and object, between worshiper and the God she worshiped. She went on to say that "spouse" connoted equality, but that, to her, union with God involved a total loss of self in God—a loss of identity and a merging. Moreover, the burning presence of God left her with a sense of awe that went beyond spousal union. I noticed that as she articulated all this, she seemed to be moving deeper and deeper into contemplation, evidently very much at peace. I refrained from asking any further questions and gave her the space to bask in the light . . .

This defining of how she experienced God's love allowed Anne to understand her own spirituality in terms of mystical tradition. The language she used, the images which surfaced, and her affective state were all in keeping with the recorded experiences of the great Christian mystics. She found reassurance that she was neither "odd" nor "unique"; rather, she understood her relationship with God to be a rare gift that was dependent on God, not on anything she could wish or do to bring it about. She was left with feelings of gratitude and humility, as well as the strong desire to be open to anything her relationship with God would entail.

But while intense light, a waterscape and a woman waiting at the foot of the cross were comforting images, Anne had to remind herself that they were *only* images. They reflected her experience of God, but they themselves were *not* God. They could only point to how she encountered God at a particular point in her history; they, too, would eventually be left behind, outgrown and inadequate. To make anything more of these images would be to venerate them as idols. In writing about spiritual direction and dream work, Gerald May (*Care of Mind, Care of Spirit*) warns how an excessive attention to dreams can "get in the way" of spiritual growth:

> The means have eclipsed the end. Similar distortions can easily occur in spiritual guidance that focuses excessively on extra-sensory psychic experiences, special spiritual powers, deliverance or any other phenomena that seem especially exciting, dramatic or meaningful. (13)

These words apply equally well to the use of imagery in
direction or private prayer: images can lead us forward, but
when we seek them out as ends in themselves, when we turn
to them in the hope of receiving a "religious high," then we
are, in effect, blocking the movement of the spirit. "A helpful rule of thumb," May continues, "is whenever a spiritual
experience or the search for spiritual experiences becomes
the overriding focus of attention, things have gone astray"
(38).

Because images work on our emotions, it is easy to
desire "religious experience" instead of relationship with
God. Images can fill the void when nothing much seems to
be happening, spiritually speaking, but sometimes it is necessary to enter that void—to live with it, accept it and learn
from it. Relying on images offers comfort, yes, but it can be
an obstacle to further growth. Knowing God involves meeting that God who is beyond all images, beyond all experiences, and beyond all techniques to "draw closer."

A few months after these images surfaced, Anne experienced a dramatic shift in her prayer life. Whereas she had
previously had a strong sense of God's presence, now she felt
nothing: all desire to pray left her, as did all consolation,
especially the experience of union. She continued to be effective in terms of reaching out to others through work and
relationships, and she was able to cope with the tensions and
disappointments I mentioned earlier; at the same time, there
were no signs of depression or anxiety. She felt a sense of
loss but was not devastated by it; rather, she understood this
absence of feeling as a necessary process to deeper union
still.

For several weeks there were no images to help Anne
interpret this shift. She went about her daily work, praying
less, sleeping more, trying not to "force" her will onto God,
reminding herself that union was gift, not a commodity to be

manipulated. Then, from nowhere, an image surfaced which did indeed bring clarity. She pictured herself on a high mountaintop, lost in the clouds and in contemplation; suddenly, a very strong force—perhaps a mighty wind—pulled her from the heights down to the flat lands.

During our time together we explored the significance of this image. I invited Anne to return to the mountain and to describe all that she saw:

"I'm high, high up, close to the ice-capped summit. It's cool but not cold—in fact, the breeze is invigorating, and though I'm wearing summer clothes, I feel comfortable. There are wildflowers, even at this height—delicate blossoms of blue, white and pink that are very fragrant. There's a layer of thick clouds which obscures everything below the mountain—I can see nothing except sky and mountain . . ."

"Anne, I can see that this place is sacred to you. Can you describe how you feel?"

"Completely peaceful, completely myself, completely at one with God. Words are unnecessary—just by breathing in all the beauty, I am breathing in God. I don't want to do anything or be with anyone. I would be content to stay here forever—I feel intensely alive. Everything except this union is irrelevant. It's more real than any reality I have ever known; it's more desirable than anything else I've ever experienced. Even speaking about it is an effort . . ."

"I know this will be hard, but I want you to remember what it was like to be wrenched from the mountain."

"Violent—like being torn apart. I felt like one of those mountain flowers that had been pulled from the ground and left, roots and all, exposed and without water."

"Anne, it is time for you to ask the mountain why you can no longer stay there."

"The mountain says that I am not to be distressed, that I will return when the time is right, whatever that means."

"Ask the mountain to explain."

"It says that the right time will be when I can come and go without clinging, when I will be equally at home on the mountaintop and in the flatlands. It says that I need to live in the flatlands because there is work to do there, that my desire for the mountain is so strong that it is getting in the way of what I have to do. I am to hold the mountain in memory but not in desire."

"How does this make you feel?"

"A little more peaceful—not so disoriented, more hopeful. I think I understand the message—I so desire to be lost in union with God that I am impatient with the ordinary tasks I have to do; they feel like obstacles in my path. Perhaps I have been literally 'too lost in the clouds . . .' "

In the discussion that followed, we spoke about the archetype of the hero's return. Typically, after learning some great mystery of life, the hero leaves the place of illumination and returns to share the benefits of newfound wisdom with those who are still searching. If Moses remained on his mountain, if the Buddha remained under the Bo tree, if Jesus remained on the mountain of transfiguration, then much work would have been left undone. Both of us agreed that Anne's spiritual journey had taken her to a place of illumination; she now needed to leave this place behind her so that she too could return and bring the gift of consciousness to others.

From my vantage point, I could suggest that the hero quest is never entirely for the benefit of the hero alone but that it brings transformation to others. Anne was at first a little uncomfortable with what she considered "inflated" claims for her journey, but when she could accept them as valid, she was left with a sense of deep peace and hopefulness. The imagery gave her the courage to continue living in the flatlands and the reassurance that her relationship with God had not diminished; it had merely "shifted."

As in the previous case study, image guidance is a useful tool when a person who previously enjoyed a warm, personal relationship with God suddenly experiences absence; it helps seeker and guide discern whether the season of dryness is "of God" or whether something in the seeker is blocking God's presence. Sarah, a contemplative in her late thirties, was troubled by the absence of feelings when she prayed. Though faithful to her regular morning and evening prayer time, "nothing happened"—or at least nothing that she could experience. She tried centering herself but would invariably fall asleep; she tried reading scripture but the words meant nothing; she tried prayers of petition, gratitude and praise, but again the words seemed rote and meaningless. Though she readily acknowledged that everything in her external life was in harmony, still she questioned whether it was her busy schedule that kept God at a distance. At the same time she was aware that the strongest realities in her life seemed to be silence and emptiness; she found that she was becoming increasingly more detached from everything around her and that she had little desire to get together with her friends. We agreed that image guidance might clarify the changes she had experienced in herself.

Having led her into quiet, I invited Sarah to image herself in the time and place where she most recently felt "connected" to God, and then, when she was ready, to describe what she saw.

"I'm back in Canada, swimming in one of the lakes near my parents' home. It's summer—the middle of August—and the water is warm. I feel as though I am one with the water and the lake seems like a womb—safe, comforting, accepting. I am conscious of God's presence. The sunlight surrounds me like a halo. I'm filled with love, with gratitude. I feel alive—really "whole" for the first time in my life. I can forgive the people who have hurt me. I'm no longer going to try to change my family—or even to want them to change. Something has happened to me—yes, there's been a significant change in my life. I've finally discovered that I can go home and be myself, regardless of what the others think. I don't have to "hide" from anyone . . ."

"So this change in yourself was something you experienced on your vacation?"

"Yes. And I've been different ever since—remember my image of being encased in a stone tower? I don't think it was a negative image—I think it means that I've become immune to many of the things which used to upset me. The absolute freedom of the womb-lake was also present in that tower. But my feelings seem to have gone . . ."

"Try to concentrate on that feeling of freedom. Do any images come to mind?"

"I see open hands, outstretched. They're open to God's gifts. They're open to God's desires for me. They're open in trust and surrender. And there's fire—flames burning . . ."

"Sarah, can you say anything more about the fire?"

"The hands are still there . . . the fire is all around them . . . swirling reds, oranges and pinks . . . now white steam, a fusion of sorts . . . it's difficult to speak . . ."

As Sarah sat in stillness, I had a tangible sense of immersion in the presence she was experiencing. Her face looked radiant; she was completely relaxed. There was no doubt that she was deep in prayer, no longer conscious of my presence in the room. I waited and prayed, not wanting to interfere with the experience. Though in most cases I have found it desirable to accompany the seeker all the way on his or her journey with images, if that person reaches a place of high contemplation, my usual response is to allow for an extended period of silence, if time allows this. To interrupt the experience with questions, directions or analysis would be a violation unless I had a very good reason for doing so. I know from my own experience as seeker that I always appreciate being "left alone" when the process of image guidance has led me into a heightened awareness of God's presence. When she was ready, Sarah opened her eyes. "I feel tired—I want to end here," she said.

We processed the session the following day. The memory of the lake experience left Sarah feeling affirmed; the memory of the fire reassured her that God was with her, in spite of seeming absence. I pointed out that the open hands imaged complete surrender—even to "non-experience," and to the pain that that brought with it. "It's the surrendering that attracts the fire," I said. "It's the posture of waiting in darkness without knowing what it is one is waiting for that gives the spirit room to move freely in your life. You are where you're supposed to be—all you can do is wait for God's time to bring about another shift . . ."

In her work with another seeker, my colleague, Liz Barry, noted a similar experience of comforting Presence that was a reality for both people involved. The seeker, in this case, was a member of her religious community and a close friend. A deeply spiritual woman, Barbara had a tendency to over-extend herself and to neglect her own needs; she was giving by nature, and her role within the community intensified this characteristic. Liz had shared with her the imaging work she had been doing in some detail; enthusiastically, Barbara had expressed the desire to do some image work of her own, under Liz's direction, but she seemed to think that this might be an imposition. Liz picked up some feelings of unworthiness and noted Barbara's surprise that she would actually want to work with her.

After several cancellations because of conflicts in Barbara's schedule, they were eventually able to get together. Barbara was eager to learn more about the process and was completely open to Liz's leading. She brought with her a dream image—that of a grace-filled woman she knew who seemed to be in some kind of danger, possibly of being stabbed. She was unclear about the actual circumstances threatening this friend, but there was a look of sadness on the woman's face which haunted her whenever she remembered the dream. To Liz, the dream-woman seemed to be an image of Barbara herself—specifically, of that rich inner self which had been so neglected.

Having led Barbara through a fairly lengthy period of relaxation during which she invited her to breathe in love, protection and trust, and to breathe out fear and alienation, Liz asked her whether she had any imagery. Barbara replied that she saw a white and yellow light; the dialogue that followed went something like this:

"What are your feelings about the light?"

"I feel the warmth of being encompassed by this light."

"As you feel the warmth and security of this light, try to remember the dream-woman who came to you. See her in the light—see her in all her beauty and grace; see her in her sadness. Ask her, 'Who are you? Why do you come to me?' "

(A long pause. Liz noticed that Barbara seemed very moved. She was crying silently.)

"What does the dream-woman reveal to you?"

"She is my God-self, my deepest self. She says that I do not give her enough time. She says that I do not feel worthy enough to be in God's presence—that I avoid praying because I think others have the right to pray but that I don't. She tells me that I have disconnected myself from her—that I have betrayed her. I'm the one who is stabbing her and endangering her. She is sad because I am depriving myself of so much . . . I think of other people's needs and yet I have run from the marvelous presence of God . . . God is as desirous of me as I am of God . . . Only God can fill the emptiness in my life . . ."

"How do you feel?"

"Very peaceful, very joyful, but also sad because I have missed so much."

"Focus on the brilliant gold-yellow light. Allow it to surround you and fill you. Ask it to fill all the empty places in your life. Stay in the light as long as you want, and then we can talk about whatever you have experienced . . ."

When Barbara finally opened her eyes, her first words were, "This is really powerful!" When she focused on the light, she had found herself completely overcome by the presence of God—a presence which flooded her with warmth. There had been no need for words or for processing. Rather, she had felt "completely at home" in God, experiencing an unconditional love which assured her that she was indeed "worthy." Only during long retreats had she felt that immersed in all that was sacred and energizing. She left the session filled not only with awe, but also with the determination to make time for personal prayer.

Image guidance, then, can break through those barriers that often make God seem "inaccessible." It is not that the process "conjures up God" in the same way that some ancient spell can summon a genie, though the temptation might be to exploit the process. Rather, what is significant is that something "shifts" in the seeker. In the first place, relaxation techniques lead to a reflective state in which one experiences heightened awareness, deeper clarity and utter vulnerability. In this state one discards masks, roles and expectations, becoming as authentically "real" as is perhaps possible. As defenses are demolished, brick by brick, the seeker becomes increasingly open not only to the suggestions of the guide and to those images which surface, but also to those hidden touches by which God sometimes speaks to us: the whispers of the heart, the warmth of grace, the stirrings of the spirit . . .

As a result, prayer happens naturally and easily—not prayer of petition or dialogue or even of praise and thanks-giving, but prayer of "being." As the seeker is transported beyond the world of senses, beyond the world of speech, nothing is necessary except to be fully present to the moment. And in this moment, the seeker becomes lost in God, for this type of prayer is nothing less than mystical union.

Noting the seeker's rapture, the guide needs to wait in stillness and prayer; nothing remains to be done while God is at work—in fact, any attempts to monitor the process through questions, comments or suggestions would be intrusive. When, however, the seeker returns to "ordinary" consciousness, the guide needs to be fully present to whatever he or she desires to share. Perhaps all that is called for is an exchange of smiles; perhaps shared prayer or shared silence may seem appropriate; perhaps the seeker may need help articulating the significance of the prayer experience. For the guide, this is the time to be the humble servant, neither taking credit nor becoming distant.

4
Image Guidance and
the Discernment Process

The process of discernment is one aspect of the spiritual life in which image guidance can play a significant role. When we are about the business of seeking "God's will" in what we do, then there are different ways of listening to that will reveal itself. Chance conversations, intuitive hunches, symbolic happenings, dreams, moments of awareness and sometimes even "signs" can alert us to what God may be asking of us in a particular situation. What is primary, however, is that we really pray, "Thy will be done."

Very often we give lip-service to God's role in our lives. We speak of wanting to do "God's will" while in reality we seek only to further our own interests. We look at security, comfort and material advantage but avoid radical risk-taking. We don't even ask God to reveal what God wants for fear we won't like what we learn. Inviting God to be part of our decision making may seem folly at best; instead we plan, strategize, calculate and control, as though we know what is good for us—and we pray that God will give us what we want.

The problem is that the concept of "God's will" has received much bad press. In an effort to give comfort when

71

nothing else will work, well-meaning individuals tend to ac-credit all misfortunes to "God's will"; accordingly, debilitat-ing illness, physical handicaps and pain are all "God's will"; miscarriages, stillborn babies and premature death are all "God's will"; accidents, traumatic loss and failure are all "God's will"; and, according to this theology, war, famine, and natural disasters are also "of God." Recently a young woman who came to me for counseling confided that she was "terrified" of knowing what God wanted for her. "Why?" I asked, somewhat surprised. "Because I'm afraid that he'll want me to be a nun," was her reply. "Do you want to be?" I asked. "No," she said, suspiciously. "Then it's unlikely that God will ask that of you," I said, much to her relief.

For many of us, "God's will" is something unpleasant which we would be better off not knowing about. Like the woman in the previous example, we suspect that God's dream for us differs from our dream for ourselves. We imag-ine that we are serving God best when we do what we con-sider unpleasant, and in fact this warped way of thinking has thoroughly infiltrated Christianity. I remember hearing nuns at my convent boarding school relate how a former superior would never assign them roles they would have chosen for themselves: thus, someone with a gift for art might be given math courses to teach; someone who enjoyed biology might be designated as French teacher; someone with a passion for scholarship might be put in charge of the infirmary. The logic behind this was that by doing their superior's will, the sisters would acquire humility and discipline and would thus be doing "God's will." In reality, many of them became frus-trated and angry and were certainly not models of Christian charity. Sadly, St. Paul's emphasis on each person having unique gifts was not part of the superior's philosophy; rather, like too many Christians, she was ready to impose the cross where the cross was not needed.

When I speak about "God's will," I like to draw on the words of Joseph Campbell who equates "purpose" with "following one's bliss." For Campbell, each of us is "called" to do and be precisely what would give us the most happiness— and this usually involves recognition and acceptance of the gifts that have been given to us. In his interviews with Bill Moyers, Campbell records his reflections about those who make a lifelong habit of avoiding their bliss: "You may have a success in life, but then just think of it—what kind of a life was it? What good was it—you've never done the thing you wanted to do in all your life. I always tell my students, go where your body and soul want to go. When you have the feeling, then stay with it, and don't let anyone throw you off" (*The Power of Myth* 118). According to Campbell, by following our bliss, we "come to bliss": we encounter people and events which draw us more deeply into the experience of bliss; doors open mysteriously into deeper bliss still, and what we discover is that the waters of eternal life are right there within us. I realize that following "God's will" can involve pain and difficulties, but, like Campbell, I believe we are always called to the experience of life in the here and now, rather than only in the hereafter.

When we fully surrender to the presence of God in our lives, then we open ourselves up to startling possibilities. Grace "happens" when we desire to live out what God desires for us; grace "happens" when we learn to trust that God knows what God is doing; grace "happens" when we are so attuned to the spirit that God's will and our will become one and the same. The more we surrender, the more we come to understand that God is indeed a personal God who cares about every aspect of our lives, down to the smallest detail. Discernment, then, is not something we reserve for major decisions but a way of being in which we grow in consciousness of who we are, making our choices accordingly. The kinds of questions to which we seek answers are not only of the practical variety but also ones of a "religious" nature. We ask: How will this possibility help me to grow in my life of faith? How can I turn this situation around so that it can be a learning experience for all those involved? How can I use my gifts most fully in God's service?

Image guidance is an effective tool in the discernment process because it puts us in touch with our deepest feelings and raises possibilities we might otherwise not have dared imagine. It does not replace the more conventional tasks of observing and listening, but it supplements what we learn and, in some cases, takes us further in our investigations: we not only have the full benefit of our rational selves and of others' thoughtful input; we also draw on the world of the unconscious, tapping its resources in surprising and dramatic ways.

Take, for example, a former student of mine, Chris. When he first enrolled in a freshman writing class I was teaching, I found myself becoming intrigued. He was more enthusiastic than the other students, certainly more talented, and while his classmates were conservative business majors, Chris looked like a remnant from the 1960s. His long wavy hair hung down his back and he would study the ends as he rocked back on his chair; as the quarter progressed, I noticed less of the hair and more of Chris' sensitivity and insightfulness. During our conferences I learned that he had grown up with traditions of Wicca (white witchcraft) and native American beliefs; learning to meditate and to reverence the earth were important aspects of his formative years.

Several months later Chris began coming to me for spiritual direction. It was a painful process for him because he had to face the abrupt shattering of his childhood happiness. His mother, injured in a motorcycle accident, had survived a coma but had emerged from the experience with a dramatic personality change. Whereas before she had been gentle and caring, now she was cruel, abusive and unpredictable. There were rows all the time, and eventually the family split up. Chris and his twin brother left home in their teens, following their parents' divorce; they were able to enjoy a comfortable lifestyle because of the allowance they received. I learned that part of Chris' experience of adolescence involved dealing with a drug problem and that this had held him back in school.

One day, Chris came to my office in a state of panic. His parents were bankrupt and could neither afford to support their sons nor to pay their college tuition; they wanted them to return home. For Chris, the thought was terrifying: though his parents were now living together again, they were by no means living in harmony; much of the old sickness was still in evidence and he knew that it would be very destructive for him to return to that environment. At the same time, he couldn't afford to maintain his present lifestyle. Because his parents "looked good on paper," he did not qualify for student loans or scholarships; moreover, his artistic temperament left him feeling emotionally incapable of holding down the kinds of jobs to which students normally turn in order to pay their way through college. Above all else, he wanted to maintain his new state of heightened awareness and to continue growing.

We decided that it might be useful to use image guidance to help him remember what it had been like living at home; the point of imaginative reentry was freshman year in high school. Because I knew this would be a painful journey, I told Chris that he could bring the experience to an end if it became too difficult. I was concerned that the reentry into the past might be more than either of us could deal with in the session. With some trepidation then, and only after having laid down the ground rules, I led Chris back in time, asking him to picture himself as he was at fourteen.

The memories were, at first, hazy. Then Chris became more and more animated, remembering his home, his school, his neighborhood. Everything was clear, entirely in focus. When he studied his teenage self, however, he looked troubled; all he saw was profound sadness. I could see him grow depressed as he recalled his parents screaming at one another and as he remembered instances of physical abuse. He began to cry, choking out the words, "It's so disgusting; it's so disgusting . . . No kid should ever have to go through that . . ." But he did not break free of the experience; rather, he continued to probe even more deeply.

Then he remembered how it was his parents who had introduced him to drugs. He saw himself not only addicted as a high school student, but also purchasing drugs from a classmate for his parents' use, with their approval. He saw himself being expelled, becoming emotional once again when he recalled how his mother had betrayed his drug dealer friend to the police after his own arrest; he spoke about his many regrets over that friendship and about his inability to forgive his mother for her treachery.

There was nothing positive for Chris to focus on. I invited him to look at his teenage self and to ask him for any wisdom he might have to share with him. And the voice of the suffering child said: "You are strong enough. You were hurt, but this was long ago. You can let it go by acting and by being a whole person. You can make it on your own."

Shortly after our session, Chris announced to me his decision to establish residency in California, to work for a while, and then to start attending UCLA. Convenient or not, there was no way he was willing to pay the price of returning under his parents' roof: enough damage had been done there already.

Another student asked me if I could help her discern whether or not she should go to law school. Angela, like Chris, had been in several of my classes and had kept up the contact, coming to see me "when there was a need." Again, like Chris, she valued her inner life and did not want to embark on any career that might threaten her peace of mind or her integrity. She, too, was bright; I remember that she was always more interested in "learning for life" than in acquiring "A's" and that she had difficulty in understanding her classmates' competitiveness.

Because she did not have any concrete images and because I did not want to impose my own rather negative attitudes about law on our process, I invited Angela to image herself inside a cave where she would meet a wisdom figure—perhaps a person or an animal. What Angela encountered was a fire, burning brightly, illuminating the dark walls around it. I instructed her to ask the fire to reveal to her what would be life-giving.

She saw herself in a classroom, teaching college students. The blackboard behind her was covered with numbers, so she assumed she was teaching accounting, her present major. In response to my questions she noticed that she looked contented and that her students were responsive. She also noted that she looked thoroughly professional and "established."

I then asked her to image herself in law school. She described a scene in the law library: "I am sitting at my desk, surrounded by books, trying to study. Students are milling around me, talking and laughing. They are not interested in learning; they only want to be rich and successful. I am sickened by them . . . I am wearing my old blue suit and I begin to pick off the lint, as though I want to make myself clean. I don't want to be like them. I'm afraid that I'll become materialistic and forget my inner journey . . ."

In our analysis of the images, we were careful not to jump to conclusions too quickly. To maintain that Angela should forget about law school on the basis of the images would have been irresponsible. Instead, the images provided some insights which would be beneficial as she continued to think and pray about whether becoming a lawyer would be for her ultimate good. Certainly, the fire had raised a new option—teaching. Through dialogue with the fire, Angela had become clearer about her own gifts and was able to name them as "understanding," "compassion" and "helping others"; teaching was one profession that would draw on these particular skills. However, we both agreed that she needed to give law a chance: the images had raised "dangers" that Angela would have to face, but perhaps the very awareness of them would save her from their clutches. She needed to be open to all possibilities.

A college writing instructor with many years of experience behind him, Bill felt called to be a writer; however, even though it was something he would be good at, even though he wanted to write, he had so far been unable to put much down on paper. The result was frustration and depression. He wanted to understand what was stopping him from doing what he wanted to do. What happened through the process of image guidance was more than either of us had bargained on.

Bill had brought no images with him, simply a question. I invited him to place himself in a room, with paper, reference books, and word processor, and to see what he was writing. After a few minutes of silence, Bill began to dictate an entire story. At first two sentences came: "Once upon a time there was a princess dressed in black who rode upon a black horse.

She was protected by a white light . . ." Then, after a few more silent moments, the rest of the story unfolded:

"The princess set out upon her horse for a distant castle. There she encountered a terrifying witch who had imprisoned many travelers in the dungeons where they had rotted to death, forgotten by all save the rats." (At this point, I noticed that Bill's expression was a mixture of fear and hopelessness.) "The princess had three options: she could retreat, but that would be a kind of death; she could fight the witch and possibly be defeated; and she could possibly win, but this would also be a death because the castle was empty and threatening and the princess would have to live in it alone."

Bill stopped abruptly, unable to go on. It seemed that he identified so closely with the princess that he couldn't bear to see what the outcome would be. At this point I intervened, instructing him to dialogue out loud with the witch. "Who are you, witch?" he asked. "I am your lack of confidence, your fear of success," came the reply. "I am your fear of what is going to come next, and this is why you cannot defeat me."

I then invited Bill to imagine the castle transformed. He saw the princess dressed in green, living in a luxurious setting. There were rich tapestries, stained glass windows and exotic carpets; there were people feasting at a table near a large fireplace. Musicians, clowns and tumblers entertained the guests, and fat dogs slept contentedly near the hearth. "But this can't be mine," said Bill.

Again, I had him speak to the witch. "Fullness can be yours if you find your own voice," said the witch. "What *do* you want to say, Bill?" I asked. He spoke of wanting to let people know that they cannot live without each other, that all are connected; he wanted to urge people to show concern for one another. I asked him to name those who listened to his voice; he spoke of himself as teacher, brother, son and friend. As teacher he asked questions rather than made statements; however, he conceded that his own voice was in the questioning. As son he had never been listened to, especially by his mother; I sensed his pain as he revealed this. Some of his siblings listened to him and his friends certainly did.

I brought the image work to a close with words of reassurance: "You already know your own voice," I said. "Wait for the words to come and receive them as a gift. Don't try to control them or to silence them but simply let them be. Don't worry about success or necessarily being heard: simply welcome them, nurture them, and share them when the right time comes . . ."

On another occasion we used a dream image to work through similar themes. Bill had a dream which reminded him of a dream that had come to him five years earlier. He was a gray rat in a barrel, swimming around frantically, struggling to get out. From the water he could see the sky, but the water level in the barrel was too low for him to be able to climb out successfully.

"How did you get in the barrel in the first place, Bill?" I asked.

"I was in a tree—on a branch—and I wanted to get down, but I was frightened of a painful fall to the ground. Instead, I decided to jump into the water because the landing would be softer."

"Ask the rat how it feels to be in the barrel," I instructed.

"Rat, how does it feel to be in the barrel?" said Bill out loud. "He says he feels trapped, there's no way out. If I stay in the barrel, I will die; but I think I will die if I leave."

"Do you want to leave?"

"Part of me does, but part of me wants to stay. I could have asked it to rain so that the water level would rise, but I'm frightened to. Instead, the water keeps on evaporating and I sink lower and lower in the barrel and can see less and less of the sky."

"I know the idea of leaving is scary, but could you try asking it to rain? Even if the barrel fills with water, you don't have to leave; you can choose to stay if you wish."

"Rain, please come; please fill the barrel . . . Now there are torrents of rain and I find myself swimming over the side of the barrel and falling into the mud. The fall is soft. I'm not hurt in any way, but I don't want to move from the barrel. It seems safe . . ."

"Bill, the barrel was like a womb for you—it was dark and nurturing, a place of development, but it's time for you to move on, into the light, into new life. Ask the barrel for its blessing, so that it will give you the courage to lift yourself from the mud and take your leave."

The barrel instructed Bill to lie down in the mud. Bill was conscious of a great radiating light and tremendous energy. As he lay there, I asked him to image himself doing whatever he most wanted to do in life, to see himself following his bliss. Bill saw himself as a writer, living in New Mexico, surrounded by a creative community. I brought the session to a close by inviting him to reexperience the energy so that it would empower him to move forward. Afterward, when we processed the session, we focused on the symbols of transformation present in the experience: birth, water and the rat himself (rodents are often associated with transformation). Bill's unconscious had spoken to him very clearly: he needed to follow his bliss, in spite of the risks involved, or his life would dry up.

Juanita is another person with whom I have worked on issues of discernment. For years, while her children were small, she had taught part-time at a local college. Her schedule fitted in well with family obligations; it also gave her the luxury of "time alone." Though some of this time was spent on running errands and doing housework, she scheduled her day so as to allow for extended periods of prayer and for such artistic pursuits as calligraphy, pottery and painting. Reading and playing the piano were also a regular part of her day. When the children were all in high school, she realized she would have to increase her income so that they could start saving for college expenses. She was offered a full-time position at the college, which she accepted.

But while her new job description and salary would meet her needs, Juanita felt uneasy. She described having panic attacks during which she would dread the beginning of the academic year. When I asked her what she was afraid of, she said she thought it had to do with the possibility of being swallowed by her job which was, in fact, going to be fairly demanding. I invited her to see if there were any images which could clarify her fears. She closed her eyes and allowed herself to freely receive any images which came.

"I can see desert sands—gently rippled, almost smooth—silver sands, gleaming under the moonlight. It's a beautiful desert—cool and peaceful. There are no people in the scene—only the sand, but I feel as though I am there, in the picture."

Her face reddened, and she continued.

"This is embarrassing—the image is becoming obscene now. The desert is being churned up by a perky phallus which pokes up through the sand like the periscope on a submarine. And it's churning up the sand with great vigor. The day grows warmer; moon becomes sun . . . That's about it . . . there's nothing more, but perhaps that's just as well . . ."

Our discussion left her feeling more comfortable about the image. The moonlit desert sand seemed to represent her feminine side and the world related to this—home, the arts, solitude, contemplative prayer . . . The phallus seemed to stand for the masculine energy that her new job would be calling for: more activity, longer hours, more responsibility at the institutional level, greater visibility . . . The important revelation was that she would need to keep both in balance if she wanted to avoid "spiritual rape"; in some form or other she would need to preserve "time alone" on a daily basis. Armed with this knowledge, she was able to begin her job with greater peace of mind; on a practical level she was able to find strategies for "self-survival" which she could work into her schedule.

In each of the cases outlined here, different dynamics were in operation: Chris needed to reenter the past so that he could discern whether or not to move in with his parents; Angela needed to see herself in different career environments so that she could more readily make a choice about future; Bill needed to let the voice of creativity sound through him so that he could see his own issues more clearly and thus respond to the invitation to write; Juanita needed to know what it was she was frightened of losing so that she could preserve what was life-giving. None of the seekers had come in with pre-conceived expectations. We simply allowed to happen whatever happened, trusting that there would be some wisdom in it.

There was little mention of "God" or "God's will" in our discussions; rather, we spoke about what would be "authentic," "life-giving," "meaningful." God was the "unspoken" reality in our explorations—present whether we were speaking about frightened princesses, ogre parents or self-seeking students, present because we were looking through the lens of truth. In each instance we examined what it means to follow one's bliss, and in each instance that was a profoundly "religious" experience.

5
Image Guidance and Healing

There was a time not so very long ago when people only recognized their need for healing if they were ill or if they suffered from some kind of disability. Suffering was equated with physical symptoms or with tangible loss. People met misfortune with stoical acceptance, observing set times for grieving in the event of a death, and "making the most" of difficult circumstances. They simply got along, as well as they could, just as their parents and grandparents had done before them; to do any less was considered self-indulgent and inappropriate. Few understood the need to heal the invisible wounds each of us carries around with us; few understood that inner hurts can be more debilitating than outer hurts and that, in fact, without healing, they can actually *cause* physical distress. Accordingly, fear, shame, resentment, frustrations, guilt, low self-esteem, anger and painful memories remained buried within.

Today we are much more likely to recognize our symptoms and to seek help than were our ancestors. With the popularization of psychology, one does not need to be college-educated to understand such concepts as "co-dependency," "addiction," "obsession," "compulsion," "denial," "behavior modification," "regression," "narcissism," "passive aggressive behavior," "inflated ego" and so forth. Through psychotherapy, self-help groups and the ever-growing market of psycho-spiritual literature, we are able to deal more and more rigorously with whatever emotional baggage we may carry with us. And since our world has disproportionately more stress than the world known by previous generations, it is good that we take advantage of every means to health at our disposal.

To suggest that our ancestors did not have their own share of incompleteness would be naive: for as long as there have been relationships, there have been emotional burdens to carry, whether or not these burdens were acknowledged or discussed openly. What is different in terms of our situation is "degree." The stability and predictability of life in the past tense are foreign to our age. The pillars of family, church and state have proved to be clay-based. Where faith and trust once served, now exist doubt and cynicism; where community support once "held things together," fractured families are scattered across continents. And religion no longer holds "the answers"; instead, it—specifically, its representatives—is often a source of scandal and confusion. In addition, we have to contend with a complex web of threats which come in forms as basic as our sources of food, water and energy, and which threaten not only the individual but also the very existence of the planet. Little wonder that our sickness has become more mortal, more in need of the healer's art.

But our hidden wounds are often so deep within that we don't even know they are there. Even after years of inner work, we have difficulty identifying them, let alone allowing them to develop scar tissue. Images, however, whether presented in dreams or in waking, offer clues from the unconscious which can assist us in our quest for wholeness. Under the care of a skilful healer, they can lead us to diagnose our symptoms, to make connections, to detect patterns of behavior—and perhaps to find a cure.

A Protestant minister—we'll call him Ralph—was struggling with some painful mid-life issues. The son of a minister whose own father had also been ordained, Ralph had grown up in a strict but loving household. From an early age, he had learned how to be a credit to his family: how to be conscientious, morally upright, helpful and pleasant—in short, "the pastor's son." These traits had served him well in his own ministry. Suddenly, however, seeming chaos interrupted what had been a comfortable lifestyle: his father died, his mother developed Alzheimer's, his daughter went off to college and his wife received a promotion which involved her being largely absent from home. Stability became a thing of the past; Ralph felt personally diminished and out of control. Someone suggested that the past—particularly his relationship with his mother—had a stranglehold over him.

Over a period of several sessions, we discussed different aspects of Ralph's situation—his deep loss over his father's death, his sense of guilt that his mother was in a nursing home in a distant state, his embarrassment at becoming more emotional . . . My intuition told me that all this suffering was not coincidental; I believed that Ralph was in a "threshold place" and that understanding the pain would take him to amazing growth and even more effective ministry. Finding an image to express all that he was experiencing would help both of us know what the next steps should be.

I invited Ralph into silence and relaxation; I instructed him to wait in emptiness until he saw an image of himself, and then to let me know what he saw. Our dialogue went something like this:

"Yes. It's not very clear but I see myself as an athlete— a fallen athlete."

"Can you be a little more specific?"

"O.K. I'm a football player—a quarterback running up the field with the ball. The crowd is standing and cheering—everyone is clapping. And then—one of the players hits me in the back—a foul!—and I'm down, still clutching the ball."

"How do you feel?"

"Lousy. It's not fair—I was doing my part and doing it well and now it's all over. I can't move—it's as though I'm paralyzed. The pain is terrible. There's nothing left anymore . . ."

"Do you see anything else?"

"Yes. I'm over on the sidelines now, off the playing area. It looks as though I'm cheering the others on."

"So you still have a function?"

"Very much so—I'm no longer the center of attention, but I'm coaching the others. I no longer have to be the one making the touchdowns."

"What about the pain?"

"I can't really feel it—perhaps it's gone. Perhaps I let it go when I let go the ball. But it still seems unfair—I enjoyed being a football star."

"Focus again on the image of the fallen athlete—the image of the football player lying in the dust. See the football player's anger. See his disappointment. See how his body is twisted in pain. See how tightly he is clutching the ball. See his tears of frustration. See how alone he is, how insignificant he feels . . . When you are ready, ask God to give you an image of healing and spend as much time with it as you want . . ."

(*A silent pause*)

"I see Jesus, kneeling in the dust, holding me . . ."

The experience not only put Ralph in touch with his pain, but also with its causes. The only son from a well-known Germanic family, he had always prided himself on his efficiency and on his effectiveness; he had never failed at anything and had never, until the death of his father, experienced any significant loss. Like the fallen athlete, his male ego had been brought low. Because he could not control the circumstances in his own life, he saw himself in defeat; he could no longer rely on his own strength, so he felt that the future had little to offer him. He realized that his sense of perfectionism made him feel guilty about his apparent weakness and that he still "held on" to the Sunday sermon as a time for him to prove his skills as pastor.

But the image was not just a negative one. Through conversation we saw that it reflected where Ralph was at a given moment in time (in the dust) but that it invited him to recognize the Lord's presence in that place. The fallen athlete could learn and grow *because of* the suffering. By surrendering to events beyond his control, by asking God to use these events to teach him whatever lesson he needed to learn, he *could* move forward—not to center field, perhaps, but to a useful place on the sidelines. By letting go of the ball, the athlete could make room for whatever future God had dreamed for him.

We spoke of mid-life as a time of transition—a time for accepting personal limitations and for letting go of ego-needs. We spoke of the new ways of ministering which can surface when one is no longer struggling to "be perfect" or "effective," but simply focuses on the work at hand. We spoke of the childhood patterns of being which may serve us well at some stages of development but which may hold us back when we grow older. Being "the dutiful son," for example, was appropriate when Ralph was an adolescent but it had begun to haunt him since his mother's illness: tapes of "you should" played constantly whenever he felt too much time had elapsed between phone calls or visits.

The image, then, brought understanding and comfort.

Ralph was able to identify some of the attitudes which had been operative and to see where they had come from. He no longer felt ashamed of his weakness, but knew that he could grow from it if he allowed God to be his strength. And he looked forward to discovering what ministering "from the sidelines" would mean for him. The journey, as he saw it, would involve claiming more of his feminine side; ironically, as our session drew to a close, another image appeared without warning: that of a pregnant woman, about to give birth.

Through image guidance, Ralph was able to make sense of the present turmoil in his life. His situation did not involve the identifying of deep wounds carried since childhood; rather, the challenge was to look at mid-life experiences and to see the ways in which he could grow. There was pain—yes—but it was not a burden which was destroying him in any way. True, he suffered from depression at times and had turned to a chiropractor to find relief from backaches, but he was basically able to function, and to function well. Our work together was enriching and empowering, but did not involve a dramatic process of healing because this was not necessary.

In Maria's case, however, the situation was very different: an artist in her early forties, she had been forged by a lifetime of pain. This, however, was not readily apparent: beautiful, articulate and vivacious, she was fun to be with and a source of wisdom to her friends; she was multi-talented and extraordinarily energetic. There was an aura of "healthiness" about her, perhaps because she took her own spirituality very seriously. Heavily involved in parish work, she kept up with her own interests while being present to her husband and five children. In short, Maria evoked both amazement and envy.

Then the unthinkable happened: Maria became a shell of herself. She seemed acutely depressed, but did not want to see her friends or carry on with her usual activities. She put on weight and began seeing a therapist. Gradually she became more conscious of the details of her own story; the more she learned about herself, the less she was able to function. The catalyst was a comment by a workshop leader who observed that her feelings "were encased in stone." That one statement was to destroy the illusion of happy family memories that had previously energized her.

Courageously Maria began to strip away the layers and layers of unreality with which she had protected herself. There was her father's suicide when he was forty and she was still in high school; he had taken an overdose of sleeping pills, but the family told everyone that he had died of heart failure. There was the death of her baby brother who had accidentally drowned in the swimming pool when Maria and her siblings, all small children, had been left "in charge" for a few minutes; her memory of this tragedy was the silence that followed it—it was never explained, discussed or processed in any way. The children—and Maria in particular—had been left feeling responsible, even though it was their nanny who had left them unattended. There was the discovery that her mother—an immigrant from a highly conservative culture—had been forced into a marriage she did not want after being abducted by Maria's father. There was her brother's death, also at forty, of cirrhosis of the liver, caused by alcoholism. Then there was the realization that she and her sisters had been molested as children, but had never been able to talk about it . . .

I was friend, not therapist. I felt numb as I listened to Maria's story, in bits and pieces, over coffee, during walks or sometimes on the telephone. I absorbed installment by installment, wondering how she could bear to carry the burden of so much pain, but knowing that naming it would ultimately bring her life. I encouraged her in her inner work, listening to her account of therapy sessions and of new insights she had gained. I prayed for her and I suffered with her. I also described the process of image guidance and offered to work with her if she thought it would be helpful.

Maria's journey toward inner healing was already well underway when we were able to spend some time together with images. I was a little concerned that there would be some role confusion since she already had both a therapist and a spiritual director; my intuition told me, however, that working with images might help her speed up the process of healing—not by creating a "band-aid effect" or by skipping necessary stages of grieving, but by helping her listen to her unconscious more deeply.

Maria brought no images with her, only pain. "Talk," I said. "Tell me anything you can remember about childhood—don't worry if you've said it before. Try to give me pictures: What did you look like? What did you play with? How did you spend your time?" She remembered her mother's fetish about cleanliness—how she would be scrubbed so hard that her skin was left raw, and how both she and her sisters were drilled to be meticulous about their appearance. She remembered her horror of dirt and her insistence about repeatedly washing her hands, especially if she had touched an animal. She remembered wearing beautifully starched dresses that never had a wrinkle in them because there was always a maid to put her in a new dress should her clothing get the slightest crumple. She remembered how she was never allowed to have a hair out of place, even when she played, because young ladies were always presentable. And she remembered her favorite doll: this she had kept wrapped in tissue in a cardboard box; from time to time, she would take it out of the box to look at it, but never to play with. It was entirely unblemished.

"We have our image," I said triumphantly. Maria looked surprised. "The doll," I said. "It's just like you! Would you be comfortable using this as our starting point?" I led her back in time, into the nursery. I invited her to take the doll out of its box and to look at it carefully. I told her to concentrate on the image and to think of nothing else. The tears rolled down her face.

"Why are you crying?" I asked.

Still with her eyes closed, still concentrating intently, Maria described what she saw. "The doll is fragile and beautiful—there's not a scratch or a bit of dirt. She is wearing white lace clothes—layers and layers of them. And there is so much tissue paper to protect her . . ."

"How is the doll like you, Maria?"

"She has no feelings—she cannot play, she cannot run around, she has no freedom. She is a closely-guarded ornament who belongs in a display cabinet or in a box. She cannot be exposed to the air or she may get ill. And she cannot speak—she cannot say what is in her heart. She cannot talk about her pain and confusion. She must pretend that everything is fine. She must not let people know the family has any secrets. She must smile and laugh, hiding everything under the lace and the tissue . . ."

I let her cry, resisting the impulse to hug her or give her a kleenex. I wanted to bring her back gently. Slowly, firmly, I began to speak:

"The doll is like you, Maria, but you have already grown beyond her. The doll is encased in stone, but you have begun your journey toward wholeness. It's a painful journey and you are bravely reliving many feelings that have been buried. Each feeling hurts, but it has a gift to give you. Each feeling will teach you how to remember, how to forgive and how to hope. Each feeling will strip away a layer of tissue, a layer of lace. And you will find healing: you will tell your story and bring others to healing also. You will tell your story until it no longer hurts . . ."

I invited her to pray with the image and then to open her eyes whenever she felt comfortable doing so. As we sat there together in the silence, I felt immense gratitude surging through me. There was a spirit of peace in the room and I knew, without Maria having to tell me, that the doll image had been a source of revelation. Her expression, when she opened her eyes, was radiant; her eyes shone through the tears. We processed what had happened, each of us amazed at the power the image had held. My "homework" for Maria was for her to return to the doll image on her own, as often as possible. I suggested that she could image herself dirtying the doll, chipping her porcelain body, even breaking off a limb or two; then, when she was ready, Maria could try putting the doll back together again—she could image washing and mending the clothes, patching the cracks, gluing on missing pieces until she was whole. The scars would still be there but they would be visible scars—trophies, almost; and the doll, covered in bandages and patches, would still be beautiful. She would no longer need a box to hide in. For Maria, this was one of the most difficult assignments of her life. She was finally able to break the doll with a hammer (imaginatively speaking) and found, in this act, immense relief and immense freedom. As I had thought, image guidance complemented all the other inner work Maria was engaged in.

While I have used image guidance primarily in situations requiring inner healing, I am beginning to explore its usefulness in terms of people who are chronically ill. Since I do not have a medical background myself, I will not work with anyone who is not thoroughly familiar with the illness in question and who is not under a doctor's care. Ideally, I see this application of image guidance being used by health professionals with their patients and not as a dimension of spiritual direction. However, if the illness involves spiritual issues (as many illnesses tend to do), then there might be occasion for a spiritual guide to help the seeker understand some dimensions of the illness which the medical profession may "miss." I strongly urge that spiritual guides simply "guide": to over-step one's expertise by giving advice about medical concerns could have life-threatening results. The following letters reflect the work one seeker and I have been doing together:

Dear Liz:

Funny, but when you first asked me what I thought of when I thought of my diabetes, I had always thought of the word, "diabetes." It was in yellow cartoon script with pinkish orange and blue outlines around the yellow letters. But once I thought of it as a thing, the large purple oblong blob I described popped into my mind. It was as if the diabetes unmasked itself.

The diabetes isn't a simple purple blob. It is purple in places but in other places it is brownish purple, the color of my potassium pills. Still in other places it is crusted over with a lead glass diamond finish, quite elegant.

In the process of imaging, I became quite relaxed. It was as if some of the cares I carry around had been lifted as I became more and more focused upon the diabetes. I seemed to be communicating with it rather than fighting it, and I felt all my stress leaving me, flowing out of me. I felt myself slowing down, and I felt the insulin reaction I was fighting ease. It felt wonderful to relax and, yet, focus on the diabetes.

During the imaging, I made contact in a positive way with the diabetes. I found out what it wanted. How it wants me to slow down and relax, not to let the world throw me. It wants me to stay in contact with the essential. The diabetes wants me to learn from it.

I'm still not certain of what it wants to teach me. This is coming slowly. I think it's to relax and focus on the important things. To become more people oriented. To just enjoy a day. To pare life down to the essentials. (I didn't know that diabetes could be like Henry David Thoreau.)

While I was imaging, things just kept popping into my mind. The answers and insights were suddenly there. Yet while they just flashed into my mind, I was feeling very relaxed, focused and euphoric. I felt at peace.

It was almost a religious experience. I get the same feeling of peace when I think of God and how God loves me without any angles. I've gotten the same feelings when we've talked about my Judaism.

I feel like I'm stopping the race and listening. It's not that I suddenly have the answers but imaging made me feel like I was on the right path. If I do more imaging and meditating, I know I'll feel better. Hopefully, I'll learn to live in peace with my diabetes. Maybe it wants to teach me to live with it and accept it, even when that means slowing down.

I want to do imaging again. I feel better now, just remembering the occasion. It felt so good to relax and realize that I must live, accept and love my diabetes. This means giving up some of the stress and slowing down. I always fought slowing down but now I understand it is necessary. If I can work with the diabetes, then I can stay well and I will feel whole.

There are times I think the diabetes is telling me to relax. The diabetes seems to be telling me not to stress out—that there will be an answer.

I want to relax and feel whole. The imaging taught me that. Actually, it has whetted my appetite for more. Maybe I can give something to the diabetes. Maybe, in the slowing down, both of us will gain.

Since the imaging process, I've found I want to be in control of my diabetes but I can't unless I'm working with it. Too often, it seems I work against it. Finding out what it wants will change that.

To that end, I'm drinking more water and today (Wednesday) I took a walk in the fresh air. It felt great. I also figured out I needed help with my diet and called my dietician, rather than waiting to see her on the 30th.

Imaging has helped me to become more attuned to what the diabetes needs. I want to do it again and learn more.

This may ramble a bit. But the process has helped me calm myself and express what the illness has meant to me. Just giving my diabetes a shape and color has pulled it into focus. Just knowing that it wants to teach me something, and that it's not my total enemy, is a big step for me. It still comes in spurts, but I'm starting to relax. Thank you, Liz.

Judith

Dear Liz:

It was easy getting to my diabetes this time. The blob really wants to talk to me about how it feels. It wants me to relax mostly and try to clear my life of the extraneous.

What's extraneous? The nervousness I feel about the diet, the nervousness I feel trying to explain the diet. I wish I didn't have to explain sometimes. Yet I know that people want to know . . .

The diabetes wanted to talk about the glucose machine. It wants a new one that doesn't have to take solutions. I felt two ways about this. While my monitor is intricate, it works well. Trying to find another one may involve using a medical delivery service and that scares me. I feel somewhat trapped, not knowing where to move.

The diabetes was truly perplexed about the hormones. It is, and I am, afraid to go off them for fear of a calcium deficiency. The dietician suggested staying on the hormones for the time being and I think I'll stay for a little while.

The diabetes hasn't explained to me why it has been going into severe reactions. I had one reaction that was so severe that it kept me from teaching on April 25th. It made my brain lock so that I couldn't concentrate. It started to do that again on May 7th. Fortunately, I got hold of Allan on the phone and he told me to get some protein.

For this reason, I'm going to get an insulin pump. Maybe having short acting insulin over a 24 hour period will steady it. My dietician believes that my digestive system doesn't empty on a regular basis and that this is causing me trouble. I feel that the pump may help me relax enough to calm my diabetes.

It is difficult to relax enough to make the diabetes happy. There are just so many things that need taking care of. There are things in the house and things at school. All of this is making me feel weak and tired.

I need more help imaging. If I can relax, then maybe the diabetes will calm down. I hope so. Sorry this isn't more upbeat.

Judith

Both in our sessions together and in her imaging alone, Judith was able to make contact with the "purple blob"—the diabetes—and to dialogue with it. From the dialogues came the understanding that she needed to live in harmony with her illness instead of fighting it; over and over again, the blob advised her to "slow down" and "relax." At times Judith asked the blob for its opinion on such matters as diet and medication. Though she listened to what it had to say, she always tested its responses by consulting with medical professionals and by discerning her own comfort level. As she continues to discover how she can live creatively with diabetes, Judith uses image guidance to supplement, not replace, the direction she receives from the medical establishment.

6
Image Guidance and
the Unchurched

Because much of my ministry happens on a university campus where I teach, I have been in a rather unique position as a spiritual director. Most spiritual directors tend to work out of their homes or out of retreat centers; those who go to them usually have strong affiliations with some particular faith and go into spiritual direction as a way of deepening their relationship with God. On campus, however, the situation is a little different: while there are a number of people who come to me for the "traditional" reasons, there are also those who come because they sense a void in their lives. This void—the absence of purpose, of meaning, of "God"—creates anxiety and pain. For many, merely recognizing the void is a courageous step which involves setting aside intellectual prejudices and admitting that even a Ph.D. is no help on the spiritual journey. Some, having left God behind in their childhood, want to rediscover what it means to be a Christian or a religious Jew; at the same time they are filled with skepticism and may be a little embarrassed about their quest for meaning. For them, trying to rediscover God seems much like trying to resuscitate Santa Claus: there is no guarantee that either exists, even though they desperately want to become "true believers."

The dynamics during our sessions together are understandably different from those which would take place during traditional spiritual direction. The "given" of God's existence, the "given" that God is benevolent, the "given" of prayer are initially absent; the rich symbol systems of scripture and the liturgical seasons are also inaccessible. What we are left with is pain—usually a precipitating crisis of some kind, and the desire to fill the void when all else fails. As guide I have to tread carefully. I have to assume that those with whom I am walking either know nothing about their religious tradition or that they need to "unlearn" what they were taught as children. I have to remind myself that concepts such as "grace," "free will" and "surrender" may amount to little more than a foreign language. Being a spiritual guide becomes a matter of helping the unchurched face their pain and, through it, to touch their inner depths; only then can we begin to talk about "God."

My work with one faculty member began "by accident." Seeing me struggle with several boxes of books, a colleague from the English department came to my assistance and helped me up the flight of stairs to my new office. On the way I explained that I now had a joint appointment teaching English and doing spiritual direction and retreat work for University Ministry; the need for greater privacy meant moving away from the faculty offices. Once in my new space, I showed Scott some of my artifacts—a wall hanging from Bolivia, cloth from Kenya, an inlaid cross from El Salvador, a Zen "rock garden," a native American smudge stick, framed photographs of the neolithic temples in Malta and of Notre Dame in Paris . . . "The idea," I said, "is to create a space that is as inclusive as possible. I want everyone to feel welcome." A few days later he made an appointment to see me.

Perhaps it was the neutral space that made Scott feel comfortable about contacting me; perhaps it was the fact that he respected me as a teacher and therefore felt "safe" talking to me about his situation. Either way, it was a "happy accident" that he had helped me move into the University Ministry offices; the experience has been rich for us both.

Our first meeting established context. Scott explained that he had been alienated from his Episcopalian roots since high school; he felt cynical about church in general, and while he believed in some form of higher power, he had difficulty acknowledging the existence of a personal God who really cared about him or anyone else. At the same time, there was enough confusion in his life to make him want to risk testing what this God was like. All his intellectualizing had got him nowhere; the only certainties were that his wife suffered from chronic depression, that many of the responsibilities of caring for home and children fell to him, that his own search for job security and a just salary had met with several setbacks, and that he himself felt frustrated, angry and exhausted. In short, he was at the breaking point.

Through this and subsequent conversations, I became more and more in touch with Scott's rage. He seemed angry with everyone—institutions which had let him down, his students, his children, his wife, himself . . . As I listened, I had a distinct feeling that "something" was blocking him from being outwardly successful. He was talented, capable, well-liked—and yet had suffered disappointment after disappointment in his professional life as well as turmoil with his family. I remembered a time in my own life when my inner disposition seemed to affect outer realities; that prolonged experience had taught me that when we take care of spiritual problems, external problems often take care of themselves. This, I knew, was not a theory that an intellectual would necessarily find tenable, and yet my intuition told me to risk articulating what I felt.

To my surprise, I found myself asking Scott if he had ever worked with images. He remembered drug-induced experiences during college days and agreed to try image guidance.

This was one of the few occasions when I have consciously imposed an image upon the person with whom I am working. Because the word "blockage" kept on surfacing in my own reactions, I felt that this would be a useful starting point. Scott had no image of his own, and so I invited him to image himself as a clear blue stream, rushing and gushing along until, toward the middle of his journey toward the sea, he would find himself dammed up by a pile of logs. All movement ended; the crystal clarity of the water turned to mud; water spilled over the banks, onto the bordering land. Then, when I saw that he was "into the image," I instructed him to speak to the logs and to ask them to reveal their names. A long silence followed, punctuated only by an occasional word as Scott learned the name of each log. "Hatred . . . time . . . fear . . . pressure . . . judgmentalism . . ." came the litany. The whole process took about ten minutes, during which Scott was entirely engrossed. The look of concentration on his face was unmistakable, as was the feeling of heightened energy in the room. I recall the excitement I felt as I jotted down what he said. The answers he received reflected what I already knew about him; it was exhilarating to think that he had tapped the source of deepest wisdom—the knowledge he carried within himself.

Both in future sessions and on his own, Scott continued his dialogue with the logs, approaching them one by one. He learned that though his hatred had outward manifestations, he also hated himself for not being "successful" and for not measuring up to others' expectations. He came from a family of academics who had taken it for granted that his would be a brilliant career; instead, while there had been moments of "success," Scott's career path mostly consisted of a series of part-time appointments which barely paid the bills. In spite of his energy and considerable abilities, he had reached his thirty-eighth birthday without having any real prospects ahead of him. Time was an issue not only because he was aware of aging, but because his multiple roles sapped him of time to pursue significant interests. His wife's depression left him as caretaker for everyone in the house; this, on top of a heavy teaching load, left him little time to send out resumes, investigate job options or even think about what he really wanted to do. Fear stemmed from the unknown—from wondering how he would continue to provide for his family, particularly if his wife did not fully recover. Pressure was the effect of experiencing failure, exhaustion and anxiety. And judgmentalism had become Scott's habitual stance toward life—a tendency to blame others when things did not work out because to do so seemed like the only defense.

In walking with Scott, I began to wonder whether any of his issues could have intensified his wife's condition. He himself wondered whether there was a connection between his judgmentalism and what he described as "Jean's defensive curl" when he spoke to her. "Let's find out," I said. We spent about fifteen minutes in silence, simply quieting ourselves after a busy morning of teaching and dealing with students. Then, without going through the usual breathing exercises, I instructed Scott to image Jean in one of the places where they most often spoke to each other. I asked him to note her clothing, her posture, her expression, the tone of her voice, the look in her eyes. I stressed that he should look on her with love and ask her how he could be of help.

At first Scott could hear only the sound of his own voice: "not overpowering . . . not browbeating . . . being with . . . warmth . . . strength . . . comfort . . . not expecting her to act like me." He explained that my instruction—to ask how he could be of help—was a question he usually spoke out of frustration and judgment and that it usually evoked a negative response. Until he worked through the data that surfaced in fragments, he could not move on to hear what Jean had to say. He also explained how difficult it was to be open to a real person instead of to an image of a log or a tree. The fact that he was dealing with Jean instead of with a metaphor provided the challenge of "knowing too much": there were too many sides to cover, too many memories which kept on coming into play.

His solution was to work with a vague "impression" of Jean rather than with a concrete picture of her; this gave him greater flexibility and openness. Soon, words began to come. "As though anything nice could happen . . ." he said with a half smile. "That's a line from our courtship—there was so much positive energy then. There was always the feeling that some good thing was around the corner . . ." He noted that while Jean spoke to him, her "defensive curl" was missing. "Let me go into them," he repeated, speaking of Jean's moods. "Don't let them mess up the strength you are giving me . . . Accept and don't let it get to you . . . don't let my mood affect you . . . maintain your strength though my moods . . . don't react out of discomfort . . . love me . . . hold me . . . assume things are O.K."

Again the words came in fragments. As I tried to transcribe what he said, it was at times difficult for me to know who was saying what. The pronouns seemed muddled, but the message was clear. "I need to make free space for good things to happen," was Scott's interpretation. "I need to hold back on my negative responses to her." I summed up the experience in four words: "Be with; let be."

One of Scott's concerns was his tendency toward self-righteousness, particularly in terms of the way he related to his wife. He noted how easily he became aware of the little mistakes she made, and how quick he was to tell her "I told you so" or to provide solutions from the vantage point of one who knew all the answers. He expressed his desire to stop being "RIGHT" with a capital "R" and to be satisfied with being "right." Instead of inviting him to relax, I instructed Scott to adopt a body posture that would reflect self-righteousness—to inflate himself and to wait for an image, with his eyes closed. A tall man, Scott sat up as straight as the office chair would allow, planted his feet firmly on the ground, folded his arms and jutted out his chin.

"I see an enormous puffed up hollow shell, reminds me of Shelley's 'Ozymandias'—how does the poem go—something about 'two vast and trunkless legs of stone/Stand in the desert . . . And on the pedestal these words appear;/ My name is Ozymandias, king of kings:/Look on my works ye mighty, and despair . . .' Talk about inflation. I think it's an image of myself; sitting this way, I feel like that puffed up shell. It's an uncomfortable way to be . . . Makes me wonder if I, too, will end up as a colossal wreck."

"Can you see anything else, Scott?"

"Yes, there's an ant walking toward the horizon, moving very slowly, bathed in a gentle, refreshing rain. The ant 'is'—it doesn't need to 'do' very much but it accomplishes a great deal all the same. Meanwhile, the puffed up shell— Ozymandias, if you will, or me—simply sits and expects homage. It cannot feel the rain; it cannot be touched. It's hard to the core."

"It seems that you would prefer to be the ant."

"Very much so—the ant is simple by nature. It carries on with what it has to do, but doesn't waste time passing judgment on others or feeling superior. It doesn't have to prove itself to anyone or even to itself; it is content to 'be.' "

Our analysis of the experience focused on "being" as

opposed to "doing." Scott's images revealed that his tendency to over-achieving led him to look down on those who functioned less efficiently. Jean, because of her depression, had become very dependent, and Scott resented this weakness. The puffed up shell provided an unpleasant mirror-image of his self-righteousness; the ant offered an alternative that he found appealing—one which invited him to find life by focusing on the task on hand, rather than fixing his attention on what others were or were not doing.

In our sessions together, Scott and I have not focused very much on God. For Scott, our work together has been an "emptying process" which will eventually put him in the kind of emotional readiness to make room for God. New developments in his family and in his professional life leave him confident about the future—to return to our stream image, the logs have now been hauled away and the water is flowing again.

Another faculty member—Tim—came to me with a sense of spiritual dislocation. Nothing in particular was "going wrong" in his life, but nothing felt particularly "right" either. He had no enthusiasm for anything, little energy, little satisfaction in what he was doing—though from all accounts, he was an effective teacher and a well-liked colleague. He, like Scott, had also reached his late thirties without achieving job security within the academic arena. He, too, was part-time, and while he had a girl friend and wanted a family, the idea of "settling down" was frightening. From previous conversations I had the impression that he had grown up Catholic but that the church had ceased to hold any significance for him. I also recalled bits and pieces about his family life—enough to make me suspect that there had been some degree of dysfunction. Because he expressed a willingness to work with images and because I felt that this might be the gentlest way to proceed, we began with some dream reentry work.

Rather shyly, Tim narrated a recent dream. He had seen steep steps leading down a cliff face, sheer rocks on one side, the sea on the other; on the steps were layers and layers of ancient books which made getting down the steps a precarious task. He thought the books could represent something he had neglected—reading or writing, possibly. I wondered whether they could stand for intellectual activity which no longer held meaning. We agreed to let the books speak for themselves.

I led Tim out onto the steps and tried to recreate the scene he had described, including as many sensory details as possible. I invited him to feel the wind in his hair, the salt spray on his face, and the teetering insecurity of the books beneath his feet. During this process it was apparent that he had completely suspended his disbelief and that he had fully reentered his dream. His physical reactions let me know his pain and his fear and helped guide me in terms of the questions I asked and the suggestions I made.

Testing my assumption that the books symbolized outgrown intellectual activity, I invited Tim to jettison some of the books into the sea, if that felt appropriate. Without further prompting he began to describe his efforts to clear the path. Some of the books were light and it took no effort to hurl them over the cliff face; beneath them were newer, less dusty books. Other books were heavier—so heavy, in fact, that I could see Tim wince as he attempted to lift them.

"This is painful, isn't it?" I asked.

"Yes—some of the books are so heavy that I can barely carry them. I don't want to let them go . . ."

"What hurts so much?"

"Seeing them smash against the rocks—seeing the leather bindings break and the pages tear, seeing the calligraphy smudge and the gold leaf wash off . . . I feel as though I am losing part of myself."

"What happens if you leave the books where they are?"

"Then I can't get down to the sea—the path is just too dangerous. And I can't go back up the stairs, either, because the way needs to be cleared."

"What do the books represent, Tim?"

"They are my history. They hold me back from moving forward. They keep me stuck in a dangerous place . . ."

Tim continued to dig away at layer upon layer of the books until he found ground—a depressed area, safe to sit in, that unexpectedly grew into a meadow. From nowhere a good "every day" knight appeared—perhaps representing one of Tim's ancestors, since there had been knights in his lineage. My first assumption was that the knight would be a wisdom figure, but I was surprised: instead of offering advice or comfort, the knight belittled Tim for asking how he had survived his scars. Again, pain crossed Tim's face as he flinched at the felt rejection. Almost as quickly, however, he smiled, explaining that a child was now disrobing the knight and removing his weapons. A look of joy and wonder shone on his face as he described how the child threw armor, sword and spear into the sea.

Through dialogue with the child, Tim learned that there was nothing else that needed to be jettisoned. "Pain is the way to life," said the child. "Hold onto what is life-giving, but let go of all that drags you down . . ." Tim was so deeply into the experience that I knew I would have to be gentle in the way I returned him to a waking state. Intuition told me that both the knight and the child were significant figures, that both were aspects of Tim's own personality.

"See the knight's pain," I said. "Learn from the wisdom of the child. The knight is not your enemy but one who is looking for friendship. Together, the knight and the child will give you strength. You need the knight's courage and resilience; you need the child's wisdom and compassion. Know that the knight and the child are one; together they can lead you down the steps, into whatever waters you choose. Both the knight and the child live in you. Speak to them both, ask them for their guidance, and when you are ready, you can open your eyes . . ."

I brought the session to an end partly because I felt there was resolution and partly because we had run out of time (the whole process had taken about 1½ hours). Tim seemed peaceful but tired—a little dazed by the "trip." I felt energized, fascinated and very awake in spite of fatigue which had been present at the beginning of the session. In our evaluation of the experience, both of us expressed surprise at how events had unfolded. My assumptions about both the books and the knight had been "off mark," but the images had revealed their meaning to us as they unfolded. Clearly, when left to their own devices, images could offer more than human logic could impose upon them.

In subsequent sessions, Tim and I discussed the seeming absence of "male energy" in his life. He had noticed that in much of our image work feminine imagery predominated; the knight and the child were exceptions. He found this curious, particularly as he got on better with women than with men. He felt very much in touch with his anima (Jung's term for the feminine aspect of the male self) but was conscious of the absence of strong male role models during his childhood and of the effects this had had on his adult self. At his suggestion, we went back in time to when he was a boy of about ten or eleven.

He imaged himself playing ball outside his house— playing with intensity because it was a way of distracting himself from all that was wrong with the family. While he was deeply in the image, I questioned him about his thoughts and feelings during that time in his life. He remembered how insensitive his siblings and mother had seemed toward his father, always wanting more and more, even though the money was not necessarily there. He remembered their anger toward him whenever he criticized them and how this led to his feeling alienated; often he sought refuge outside the house because he couldn't bear to be *inside* with his brothers and sisters. He remembered how bent and old his father always looked when he came home from work and how joyless he seemed to be . . .

As we explored these memories, it became clear that Tim's satisfaction with part-time work and his reluctance to settle down stemmed from his rejection of the kind of life his father led—one of hard work, no fun and little gratitude on the part of those for whom he labored. Early on, apparently, it seemed that Tim had balked at the idea of "growing up" and had resolutely decided that he just would not do it. While he was still concentrating on the image, I asked Tim how he could rediscover his male energy so that he could continue the business of growing up.

"I need to affirm myself in what I do," said Tim. "I need to go back to playing sports instead of simply watching them. I need to spend more time with my male friends so that I can get to know them more. I need to dream positive dreams for myself so that I know that I don't have to live life the way my father did . . ."

All the answers to Tim's quest for wholeness lay within himself. Through image guidance, I was able to help him identify the questions he needed to ask so that he could then listen for the response. Like Scott, he was on a spiritual journey that began with looking at life issues with complex roots. Issues of personal history, childhood patterns and present relationships needed to be clarified *before* we could move on to examining God-issues.

7
Image Guidance as a Means of Understanding the Self

The "self" is almost as elusive a concept as what we mean by "God." After all their wrestling with words and grappling with meaning, philosophers, theologians and psychologists are still unable to provide us with certainties; they have offered rich insights into what it means to be human, but, at best, their definitions about the self are merely attempts to define a reality that seems to be beyond articulation. For Jung, the "self" is the totality of the whole psyche, an inner center responsible for the process of individuation. M.-L. von Franz, in her essay "Patterns of Psychic Growth," follows Jung in suggesting that this center is "a sort of 'nuclear atom' in our psychic system. One could also call it the inventor, organizer and source of dream images" (Carl G. Jung, ed., *Man and His Symbols,* Dell, 1964). She points out that people in all places and in all periods of history have intuitively grasped the existence of this inner center, calling it by different names: "The Greeks called it man's inner *daimon;* in Egypt it was expressed by the concept of the *Ba-soul;* and the Romans worshipped it as the 'genius' native to each individual. In more primitive societies, it was often thought of as a protective spirit embodied within an animal or fetish" (162). Von Franz goes on to explain that how far the "inner regulating center" develops "depends on whether or not the ego is willing to listen to the messages of the Self," namely, through the investigation of one's dreams (163).

Neither Jung nor von Franz has said the final word about the self, but they do provide some useful groundwork: the "self"—whatever that is—is central to one's being; it is slowly but constantly evolving; it instructs us how to grow by sending us specific dream images; we are free to turn to it for wisdom or to ignore it. When we are receptive to the direction offered by the self, we find psychic health; on the other hand, when we close ourselves off from it, we run the risk of being overcome by emptiness and meaninglessness. "The anxiety of meaninglessness," writes Tillich, "is anxiety about the loss of an ultimate concern, of a meaning which gives meaning to all meanings. This anxiety is aroused by the loss of a spiritual center, of an answer, however symbolic and indirect, to the question of the meaning of existence" (*The Courage to Be,* Yale University Press, 1980, p. 47). To the extent that we live out of our spiritual center, out of our self, we will find meaning, purpose, energy and wholeness, for it is there that we can most deeply encounter the reality of God:

> The full knowledge of the Self, in the overwhelming testimony of the mystics, includes a transcendent dimension. The Self participates actively in what we have come to call God. It is of and for God (Anne Brennan and Janice Brewi, *Mid-Life Directions: Praying and Playing Sources of New Dynamism,* Paulist Press, 1985).

"Dream images," the messengers of the self, are not confined to dreams: they also surface in fantasies and in spontaneous images. And the self seems to send us other messengers—hunches and intuitive guesses, whispers and suggestions, meaningful "coincidences" . . . Through image guidance, it is possible to connect with these messengers so deeply that the integrating action of the self—or of God—is given powerful expression. This can be seen from the following case study in which Tim, one of the subjects in Chapter 6, is again the focus.

Tim, if you recall, was struggling with issues of identity and purpose. In our sessions together, we had begun exploring his childhood and the attitudes that it generated; we had also worked on his feelings of being called to "something new"—a new way of being, perhaps, or a new phase of professional life. The session I am outlining here began with four simple words which came to Tim in a dream: "SEEK A RICH LIFE."

When Tim came for his appointment, I was neither feeling well nor very conscious. A bad cold and a sick household had left me exhausted; I felt I had little to offer, in terms of either listening or leading. I begin with this seeming trivia because what happened during the session was truly amazing; it demonstrates that when the self wants to communicate, it does so, regardless of the limitations of those involved.

We began by discussing Tim's dream. In it a woman friend gave him a biography in which she inscribed the four words, followed by a definite exclamation point. That was all there was to the dream, and yet it had evidently intrigued him; he seemed energized as he spoke about it and was anxious to explore it further through image guidance. We examined the significance of the words. Tim felt that "seek" was an imperative, urging him to move beyond where he was in a spiritual sense; however, he did not rule out the possibility that outer traveling might be involved. "Rich" was again a word with inner and outer connotations. He believed that the richness that he was meant to find was within himself, but that in finding it he might discover other kinds of riches. The biography was, perhaps, a model of how he *could* live; the woman in the dream could be an "anima" figure that was instructing him to be more in touch with his feminine energy.

After our preliminary discussion, I invited Tim to reenter his dream. Tired and rather detached from the process, I instructed him to close his eyes, abbreviating the preparatory stages of image guidance. Tim, fortunately, was so eager to learn from his image and so adept at relaxing himself that he didn't seem to be adversely affected by my lack of guidance. Before I had even managed to center myself, he was already well into his dream and ready for further explorations.

Feeling rather inadequate and wondering whether we would "get anywhere," I instructed him to open the book and see what it would reveal to him. Tim mentioned the title and author, but they were not names I recognized; he then opened to a chapter entitled, "Calumny."

"Calumny. Calumny—what does it mean?" he asked.

"It has to do with lies," I said, caught off guard. "Calumny and detraction—slandering one's neighbor. What does this have to do with 'seeking the rich life'?"

"It might be what stands in the way of my seeking," said Tim. "I don't believe I have a spiritual center—or at least, if I do, there isn't much depth to it. I don't believe in myself."

"So it is your lying about yourself to yourself that gets in the way of progress?" I asked, finding myself becoming more responsive.

"Yes. It seems that the biography is to prod me to look at my own life. The dream image has begun to shift—I see myself on a path, but I can't get very far because of my poor self-image."

"So your attitude is like a roadblock—a boulder of some kind?"

"Yes—that's just what I can see—a massive rock of white granite, hand-hewn in ancient times, monolithic in scale. It reminds me of the pyramids."

As I listened, I was struck by the whiteness of the granite: white was the color of positive energy and of enlightenment and yet, up until this point, we had associated the roadblock with negative forces. Finding myself becoming more attentive, I again summarized what I had heard:

"So you want to undertake this journey but you are blocked in your path by an enormous obstacle which has something to do with how you perceive yourself?"

"Yes."

"Is there any way you can get around this block?"

"There seems to be a narrow path flanked by a sheer ravine to the right of it, but I can't get to it."

"So you have to confront the block?"

"Yes, but there's a door in it—beautifully crafted, almost invisible, no jams or hinges in sight. I am going through the doorway and I find myself in a dark place—it smells very old—as old as pre-history—and it feels sacred. I know I am standing on holy ground. I feel very peaceful, very content. I know I belong here and that others have been here before me."

"Is there anything else you see?"

"There is a torch in a bracket on a wall. Above it there is nothing but soot, but it casts its light around the interior of this vast, vast space. There is nothing on the walls, so I begin to draw an animal—an antelope of sorts. It is a primitive animal and I feel that what I am doing is immensely significant."

"So you feel you have a purpose? You feel peaceful and connected? You are doing something holy? You feel connected to your ancestors?"

"Yes. I know who I am and what I have to do. I experience incredible energy and strength. I am not afraid."

"You look very joyful."

"I *feel* joyful. This space, this vast, vast room, is inside me and outside me at the same time. I have discovered there *is* depth to me, a richness inside. What I am seeking is right inside myself—it only becomes a block if I ignore it, but when I explore its depths, then I find what it is I am looking for without having to go anywhere."

"What about the biography? Does it hold any more wisdom for you?"

"No—it's irrelevant, now. I don't need to learn from someone else's life—it is my own living that I have to concentrate on . . . There's a shift in the image. I am on the other side of the granite square, having exited through another door. I am ready to continue my outer journey, wherever that may lead me, but I can return to the inner room whenever I want to—I know how to enter it . . ."

"What you have discovered is the place deep, deep within yourself, that place which is the source of all wisdom. You can return to that place whenever you want. You can go back, remove the torch from its bracket, and explore every wall, every corner, every inch of ceiling and floor. You can go back and, with the light of your torch, continue to draw sacred drawings and to see drawings that others may have done. Thank the granite block for everything it has revealed to you; repeat to yourself everything that you have learned, so that you may carry this wisdom away with you. Then, when you are certain that you will remember all that you have learned, open your eyes . . ."

When we were ready to process the experience, both Tim and I were conscious of the energy in the room. For Tim the granite block had been more "real" than anything he could touch—than anything out on the street, for example, or anything within my office. He felt "changed" by this reality, more conscious, more alive, more hopeful. For my part,

I too was awake. The more Tim had entered his image, the more I felt drawn into it. I too could see the interior of his granite block; I too could smell the must of ages and see the primitive cave drawings; I too felt as though I were standing on holy ground. The sluggishness induced by cold medicine had worn off and I experienced the heightened awareness that always comes when I am in touch with my own depths. There were tears of joy in Tim's eyes as we talked about what had happened and the implications it held for him. Fear, self-doubt and self-deprecation had vanished; "calumny" was a word of the past.

I brought the session to a close by making some suggestions for Tim to follow on his own. One was that he should return to the granite block by himself and continue his explorations; to this end, I described several techniques for him to follow (see pp. 36–38) to help him with relaxation, process and evaluation. I also suggested that he could consciously invite God into this inner space to accompany him in his adventure so that this temple of his could become the place where he worshiped. There he could ask God to reveal how he could find "the rich life" the most fully and to be his guide along the way.

The next day—today, in fact—brought me a new "core experience" when another seeker asked me to help her deal with "self issues." As I write this, I am conscious of my own heightened awareness and increased creativity; even after a two-hour session, even after getting supper and putting away groceries and dishes, even after interacting with family members and nursing my ongoing cold, I still feel exhilarated. The energy which keeps me going is my determination to commit to paper what I recall of the experience while it is still fresh.

The seeker is a woman in mid-life who is haunted by parental issues. After years of therapy, she has become aware of her hostility toward her mother, of her own poor self-image and her confused feelings about her father who died about fifteen years ago. Desperate for healing, she asked me to use image guidance to help her understand why she felt physical revulsion toward her mother and yet, at the same time, saw much of her mother in herself. She treasured her memories of her father but wondered whether perhaps she could have been molested as a child because of some of the "vibes" her mother had communicated at the time. She remembered distinctly how she had always been "Daddy's little girl" until puberty, when he seemed to push her away. She also blamed herself for his death because she had left home against his wishes and he had died shortly after her return, a year later.

Her request felt like rather "a tall order": I wasn't sure whether the process of image guidance could accomplish all this. At the same time, I was aware of my own excitement at the challenge and knew that the information the session generated could be invaluable in terms of my own research. This in itself was something to be cautious of. I explained to Cara that for the process to "work," I had to abandon my intellectual curiosity and any desire I might have to "write up" what happened. I needed to sit with her prayerfully, not in a way that was self-serving; I needed to remind myself that I was only a "channel" for whatever God wanted to happen and that I was serving God, not my ego. Given the success of the session with Tim, abandoning myself to the "flow" of whatever happened might be more than I could handle. For her part, Cara was afraid of what the images could reveal. She was especially afraid of learning that her father had indeed molested her; she knew that the potential for pain was strong.

Given the concerns each of us felt, I asked if we could pray before we got started. I was more afraid of my own desire for "knowledge" than about Cara's inability to handle the pain. Articulating my concerns, both to Cara and to God, helped me find my center and to feel that I could set aside my vested interests. I then invited Cara to trust that her deepest self would reveal whatever was necessary for her growth, however painful that might be; I reminded her that we could stop the process whenever she desired.

There was no specific image to begin with. Drawing on what Cara had said about family life, I asked her to see herself in all her beauty and in all her vulnerability and then to describe what she could see.

"I see myself as a young child, playing with my father. He is pulling on my thumbs and we are giggling. I can feel the stubble of his beard and I remember the comforting smell he had. I feel safe and loved. I miss him . . ."

"So your father was someone who played with you—you are not afraid of him, or of being close to him. Cara, I know this is painful, but try to image your mother in the picture."

"She is standing in the doorway, but she keeps on turning away. She doesn't want to look."

"Why?"

"I don't know."

"Ask your mother—aloud, if you feel comfortable—why she is upset."

" 'Mom, why are you upset?' She won't answer."

"Invite her to join you."

"She says she can't—she has too much work to do."

"Ask her—again, aloud—what she wants you to do."

" 'Mom, what do you want me to do?' She says she wants me to go to sleep and she wants Dad to go to sleep. She doesn't want us to play."

"How does your dad feel?"

"Well, he ignores her but he stops playing with me—he no longer wants to be close to me because of what mom might think. I want *her* to go away because she's taken my joy away. I didn't kill my father—*she* did, by not giving him any affection and by not letting the two of us be alone together."

"I can see you are very angry."

"Yes, I hate her. All the time I thought I was the one who was in the wrong—I thought it was wrong to love Dad so much, I thought he had hurt me, but she hurt both of us and now she keeps on coming to stay with me like a shadow I can't get rid of. I walk like her, I have her mannerisms, but I can't stand her. When she comes, I try to keep her busy so that I won't have to talk to her—and I don't want to touch her. My biggest nightmare is that she'll get ill and I'll have to nurse her. And I hate how she makes herself 'useful' and how she keeps on asking me questions about what I'm doing . . ."

"Cara, why are you afraid of your mother?"

"I'm afraid she'll take away my joy like she did with my father. I have felt real joy in the last year—a real sense of satisfaction with what I'm doing and I don't want her to rob me of it."

"It sounds as though your mom is trying to get close to you."

"Yes, perhaps she thinks she can get close to dad by getting close to me."

"Ask your mom if there is anything she wants to tell you."

"She is saying all kinds of things but I am not listening—there's nothing but confusion."

"So she is trying to communicate but you are blocking her out?"

"Yes, and people think I am cruel to her. I was close to my Aunt Doris, her sister, but she has distanced herself from me because of the way I treat mom. I feel I have lost both her and mom."

"It sounds very much as though your mother *is* trying to

get close to you, but it is also clear that you have many reasons to be angry with her. Cara, she no longer has any power over you. She took away your joy when you were a little girl, but you are no longer a child. You are a grown woman and no one can take away your joy. The joy you feel is God's gift to you and God will protect it. You see yourself through your mother's eyes: remember that she was jealous of you because she didn't know how to play and that she didn't trust you or your father. Try to see yourself through your father's eyes: remember how precious you were to him and how much joy you gave him. Know that you *are* beautiful and that you *are* good. You are neither your father nor your mother but your own unique self, uniquely mirroring the God who made you . . ."

When we processed the session, Cara cried. "I don't feel any joy," she said. "I can't forgive her." Words came to me, seemingly from nowhere. I said that she was confronted with a situation in which two needs conflicted: her mother's need for forgiveness and intimacy and her own need for distance and self-preservation. She could turn away from her mother but something would harden within; she could, on the other hand, "open the door" and perhaps there would be transformation. Either way there would be pain, and only she could decide which kind of pain she wanted to live with. I suggested that she should ask her father to be present to her—that she should thank him for the gifts they had shared, asking him to help her forgive her mother, just as she knew he had done. I also asked her to pray specifically for God's guidance, so that she would be able to do whatever she was being called to at this time.

It was a difficult, emotional session, and yet the word I used earlier was "exhilarated." I was very conscious of the wisdom welling up in both Cara and myself. As I listened to her dialogue with her images, I knew intuitively where to go.

I had no reason to focus on her mother so intensely, but the word "jealousy" came to me and I listened to it. Also, as I allowed myself to get into the scene of child playing with father, I felt only positive energy, and this directed me to believe that the relationship had been good and wholesome. My impressions of the mother, however, were of a deeply wounded woman who withdrew her affection from child and spouse because she did not know how to give it. I identified this lack of feeling, together with her suspicions about incest, as the primary reason for Cara's own feelings of inadequacy. Cara's tears came from a very deep place but I was not afraid of them nor of the pain that had been unleashed. Again, whatever source of healing was speaking to my inner depths reassured me that these tears would bring relief and empowerment. Like Tim, Cara had journeyed into her inner center, and what she found there was very good; as guide on the journey, I too found my way into the center and there received clarity, peace and the gift of humility.

Appendix
Working on Images of Self

Create a "collage" about yourself. It can be pictorial, that is, it can consist of photographs, maps, drawings, postcards, certificates and anything else that might reflect something of who you are. It can also be an "object" collage consisting of items you associate with yourself (a flower, for example, if you are into gardening, or a pair of goggles if you swim). Study the collage in silence; if you are working with an object collage, feel each of the items slowly, taking in sense impressions about each object and reflecting on yourself as owner. Close your eyes and ask for an image of yourself to appear. Concentrate on the image and watch it in action. Ask the image specific questions, for example:

- Why have you come to me at this time?
- In what ways do I resemble you?
- What qualities do we share that are life-giving?
- What qualities do we share that I need to change?
- What wisdom do you have to share with me?

When you feel you have learned all that the image has to teach you, thank it for its help. Upon opening your eyes, journal with the image to see if you can extend the experience or make any new connections that may have escaped you.

*   *   *

Find a baby photograph of yourself—one that strikes you in some particular way. Perhaps there is a look of innocence that is appealing, perhaps the child looks contented and well loved, perhaps there is a sadness about the child . . . Study the photograph carefully, focusing your attention on the dominant quality that led you to select that photograph. Now look at a recent photograph of yourself, again selecting it because of some unique quality. Pay attention to the ways in which you have changed physically. Then ask yourself the following questions:

- What have I gained by growing up?
- What have I lost?
- What do I miss that I had as a child?
- In what ways can I retrieve the child I once was?
- In what ways am I still childish and immature (as opposed to childlike)?

Using the answers to these questions as your starting point, allow your adult self to dialogue with your child self. Placing a pen in each hand (use your left hand for the child if you are right-handed and vice versa), record what each has to say. Do not censor any of the material, either for spelling, grammar or content.

*   *   *

Whether you have any artistic abilities or not, dare to create a portrait of yourself. Using any medium—paints, play dough, plaster casts, crayons etc.—try to capture something of who you are in concrete form. Allow your hands to provide the shape, not your head. Do not try to create a masterpiece; rather, let the truth of who you are speak through the medium you select. When you have completed the project, focus your complete attention on this image of yourself. What do you see?

* * *

Choose a record, tape or disk (without lyrics) that you listen to frequently and find moving. Listening to the music in an uncluttered space, give yourself the freedom to dance in whatever way "comes." Don't be concerned about choreography or awkwardness; rather, allow your body to express itself through the music and listen to what it has to say. Journal about any feelings that may have surfaced during the experience.

* * *

Sitting in front of a large mirror, study your reflection for at least ten minutes. Pay attention to the expression in your eyes, to your posture and to the placement of your hands. Note whether you sit still or fidget. Ask yourself:

● What do I like about myself?
● What do I dislike about myself?
● What things can I change?
● What am I seeing for the first time?
● What truth can the mirror reveal to me?

Either in your journal or through active imagination, ask the mirror to show you who you are.

*   *   *

Make a list of all those things, people and events which make you afraid. One by one, give each a visual representation—perhaps as a goblin, a witch, a snake, a dragon or anything else that seems appropriate. In your journal, dialogue with each fear/creature that you have named. Ask them:

• What are you doing in my life?
• How is it that you have power over me?
• What can I learn from you?
• What must I do to tame you?

*   *   *

Make a list of all those things, people and events which have helped you on your journey. One by one, draw each of them, either as they appear to you or else symbolically. In your journal, thank each of them for their help. Then imagine yourself leaving them behind, continuing the journey alone. Ask your helpers:

• Where will my strength come from now that I have left you behind?
• What gifts can you give me for the journey?
• In what ways can I be a helper to others?

*   *   *

If you do not already have one, create a sacred space for yourself—a place where you can be fully yourself and where you can spend time alone and in prayer. Remove clutter. Select art work with symbolic value. Choose a place where you can sit comfortably and meditate. Soften the lighting; add a plant or two to the environment . . . When your sacred space is ready, close the door and pay attention to all the details which work together to create the right environment for you. What do these details reveal to you about yourself?

*   *   *

Taking as much time as you can, go on a vision quest. This might involve spending time alone in the woods, going out alone in a boat, camping near a lake . . . In your solitude, listen to what the natural world has to reveal to you: listen to the sound of the wind, to the rustling of leaves, to birdsongs and the lashing of rough waves. Listen, too, to the dreams and images which come to you during this time. Before closing your eyes, ask for a dream or image which will enlighten you in some way. Pay special attention to any words which you may hear during this time, whether waking or sleeping.

*   *   *

Choose an archetype that may be dominant in your life right now (examples might be trickster, magician, warrior, martyr, king, queen, hero . . .). Draw this archetype, allowing it to take shape according to the way in which you experience it. Close your eyes and concentrate on your drawing in your imagination. See if the image moves or whether it has any wisdom to share with you; ask the image any questions that may seem appropriate.

*   *   *

Wrap an empty box as attractively as you can. You may want to paint the box, create your own gift wrap, or decorate the box with shells; what is important is that you spend time and care in the wrapping and that you are pleased with the results. Take the box into your sacred space and place it before you. Tell yourself that what the box contains is your "bliss" that which will make you happy in life. Focusing on the box, think of your bliss and what it means:

• Where will your bliss take you?
• Who will journey with you?
• What do you need for this journey?
• What attitudes in you need to shift before you attain this bliss?

*   *   *

Choose a fairy tale which you know well. Remind yourself of the theme, characters and plot. Which character or characters do you most closely identify with? Through imagery, allow yourself to become one of those characters and watch yourself in action; dialogue with the character about any specific issues you may have. When you have done this, focus on the character that most resembles an antagonist or a negative aspect of yourself; again, image this character and move into dialogue. In your journal, let the characters dialogue with one another freely.

*   *   *

Work with rune stones, astrological charts, horoscopes, and other character/destiny revealing devices. How much "fits"? How much is "off the mark"? How much leaves you wondering? Journal about your experience, focusing particularly on your desire for self-knowledge.

Works Cited

Anne Brennan and Janice Brewi. *Mid-Life Directions: Praying and Playing Sources of New Dynamism*. Mahwah: Paulist Press, 1985.

Joseph Campbell. *The Power of Myth*. New York: Doubleday, 1988.

Edward Edinger. *Ego and Archetype*. New York: Penguin, 1972.

Barbara Hannah. *Encounters with the Soul: Active Imagination*. New York: Siga Press, 1981.

Robert A. Johnson. *Inner Work*. San Francisco: Harper & Row, 1986.

————. *He*. San Francisco: Harper & Row, 1989.

————. *She*. San Francisco: Harper & Row, 1989.

————. *We*. San Francisco: Harper & Row, 1985.

C.G. Jung, ed. *Man and His Symbols*. New York: Dell Publishing Company, Inc., 1964.

Stephen Larsen. *The Mythic Imagination*. New York: Bantam, 1990.

Gerald G. May. *Care of Mind, Care of Spirit*. San Francisco: Harper & Row, 1982.

Carol S. Pearson. *The Hero Within*. San Francisco: Harper & Row, 1989.

Gerald H. Slusser. *From Jung to Jesus*. Atlanta: John Knox Press, 1986.

Paul Tillich. *The Courage To Be*. New Haven: Yale University Press, 1980.